OUT OF **DEATH**
COMES **LIFE**

OUT OF **DEATH** COMES **LIFE**

TROY C. MOORE

TATE PUBLISHING & *Enterprises*

Published by Tate Publishing & Enterprises, LLC
127 E. Trade Center Terrace | Mustang, Oklahoma 73064 USA
1.888.361.9473 | www.tatepublishing.com

Tate Publishing is committed to excellence in the publishing industry. The company reflects the philosophy established by the founders, based on Psalm 68:11,
"The Lord gave the word and great was the company of those who published it."

Book design copyright © 2008 by Tate Publishing, LLC. All rights reserved.
Cover design by Jonathan Lindsey
Interior design by Kellie Southerland

Published in the United States of America

ISBN: 978-1-60696-462-0
1. Religion: Bible: Meditations - General
2. Christian Living: Spiritual Growth: General
08.10.27

ACKNOWLEDGMENTS

This is the day the LORD has made! I would like to first thank God for sending His only begotten Son to die on the cross for me. I thank Jesus Christ for His resurrection power that is still evident in the body of Christ today! Thank you LORD for all you've done for me and for putting the words in my spirit to make this book successful.

This book is dedicated to the memory of my father, my hero, Nathaniel Moore, Sr. (October 21, 1935-July 10, 1999). His death inspired me to begin these writings. I thank God that He gave his life to the LORD in the latter part of his life and because of that he is smiling now, and I pray he's proud of his son. I would also like to thank my mother, Hazel-Lee Moore, who is the backbone of the Moore family. Mom, thank you for praying for me even when I didn't know that you were praying. When everyone else gave up on me,

Momma, you were there not speaking much through your mouth, but your heart always spoke to me.

I thank God for my lovely wife. She is the woman who pushes me into carrying out the visions the LORD shows me. She is the woman who had my children. She is also the co-pastor of New Generation Ministries. Her name is Reverend Alesia Moore. Thank you, LORD, for my two boys, Dougie and Seth C. Moore. What gifts to the body of Christ! A most gracious thank you to the New Generation Ministries family, who have continued to pray for their pastors since the beginning. With an excellent group of people, it makes my job easier to lead them into glory!

I also would like to thank God for my pastor, my covering, my spiritual father, Archbishop LeRoy Bailey, Jr. God always places the right people in your life at the right time. When my biological father passed away in July 1999, the LORD strategically placed Archbishop Bailey in my life. Thank you, Archbishop. I will never forget what you have done for me and my family. I also have to mention my spiritual mother, First Lady Reathie Bailey, wife of Archbishop Bailey. I have said it before, and I'll say it many times more, the best message ever preached to me is both of your walks in ministry. Your walk speaks bountiful things, and I'm grateful for you both and your children and grandchildren. May God continue to enrich your lives through Him.

If there is anyone I left out, please forgive me. I am overwhelmed over my first book. It was honestly written through pain and suffering, all to the glory of God!

In Christ,
Reverend Troy C. Moore, Senior Pastor
New Generation Ministries
"The Church without Walls"

FOREWORD

There are two words that describe life: "Wow!" or "Woe!" This is one of those "Wow" moments described in this book. Pastor Moore shares his pain and leads each of us to gain. It is a book that frames the despair and hope within each of us. He takes us to conferences daily that we may never attend to hear from the most dynamic and powerful gurus of our time to inspire and motivate our day. These gurus and motivators are not outside of our reach, they are intrinsic to our very nature. Our death to our anger and cynicism equips us to arise a more distinguished, dynamic, and powerful person who can bring joy and fresh life to others who are in the grips of despair.

The passage John 12:24 (NKJV), "Most assuredly, I say to you, unless a grain of wheat falls into the ground and dies, it remains alone; but if it dies, it produces much grain," can possibly be the answer to a dream, vision, or decision that you have to make to have a new beginning; the beginning of a career, a business, a family, or close the chapter on all that has been debilitating in your life. Read this book and remember there is always hope, there is always an alternative and God will turn your "scars into stars." *Out of Death Comes Life!* This is a call to live, lift, and be encouraged. In every seed there is life, and you are that seed, that life-bearing source for yourself and your heritage.

Archbishop LeRoy Bailey, Jr., Senior Pastor
The First Cathedral
Author, *A Solid Foundation: Building Your Life from the Ground Up*
Whitaker House 2003

INTRODUCTION

I remember growing up in a household where domestic abuse was evident—all from the hands of my father. For many years, I truly hated my dad because of all the pain he inflicted on my mother and my eight siblings. As I grew older, I still had this hatred in my system towards my dad because I felt like I hadn't asked for the abuse and I know my mother and my siblings hadn't asked for it either. However, in 1999, the unthinkable happened. At the beginning of the year, I began to develop a relationship with my dad. I felt like a little boy whenever I was out with him; whether we were in the yard fixing cars (which was his hobby) or just taking a ride in his car. Even though I was 29 years old at the time, I felt like a child when I was with him because on the inside I could hear myself saying, "I'm with my dad and my dad is with me!" I very seldom said those words throughout the previous years of my life.

Then, in June 1999, my father became ill and was placed in the hospital. The dad that I missed during the first 29 years of my life was on bed rest. I couldn't believe it! My hero and I were now unable to go for drives together. He was unable to work his gift of being a mechanic and it was devastating to me. I was not in church and, to be honest, I didn't like God or pastors because I felt that neither was there for me through the years of domestic abuse.

On Saturday, June 26, 1999, I went to a night club and, though I was the usual life of the party, I was not myself that particular evening. I couldn't enjoy myself for some reason. Something was pulling me and I fought it the entire night. The following morning, June 27, 1999, I got out of bed and did something that I normally would not have done at that time–I went to church. I remember walking into the First Baptist Church located on Greenfield Street in Hartford, Connecticut. I remember at the end of the sermon, Pastor LeRoy Bailey, Jr. opening the altar for those who wanted to give their lives to Jesus Christ. I rose from my seat and walked towards the front of the church. That was the longest walk I've ever taken in my life. On Sunday, June 27, 1999, I gave my life to Jesus Christ! At the time, I thought that because of what I did, God would strengthen my dad so that we could continue to build our relationship. I was wrong.

I was at work one day not too long after the Sunday I received Christ as my personal Savior and LORD. I was going through my normal routine even though my father's health was getting worse. He was hooked to all types of machines in the hospital. I will never forget the day. It was Friday, July 9, 1999. My mom called me at work and told me that the doctors said my dad, my hero, only had approximately two to three days to live. I cried at work and a coworker drove me home because he was worried about me driving.

On Saturday July 10, 1999, at approximately 9:10 am, while I stood in front of his bed, my father took his last breath. Remarkably, at that time I did not cry. I actually felt peace and I remember the sun beginning to shine through the window of his hospital room. The Spirit of God strengthened me, and I even got up at the funeral and gave remarks about my dad, my hero.

And then, I sat down at a computer one day and sent out an encouraging word over email that the LORD told me to share with four people. Today, that email ministry, which is now called "LetsGo! Ministries," is being received by thousands of people all across the world. The LORD placed on my heart to name my first book "Out of Death Comes Life" because it was conceived and birthed out of pain and suffering. I truly know in my heart that my dad's death caused something inside of me to stand up and know that God had a plan for my life. The Bible says, "Most assuredly, I say to you, unless a grain of wheat falls into the ground and dies, it remains alone; but if it dies, it produces much grain." (John 12:24, NKJV).

The following devotionals are intended to reach those who have never encountered Jesus Christ in a non-traditional manner and to encourage those who currently have a personal relationship with Him. Jesus is the answer for every situation that you may go through. Through these devotionals you will be able to withstand every struggle, knowing that you are already victorious in Christ Jesus.

God bless you and I thank you for your support and prayers. Remember, God is still in control and He is always thinking of you!

THOUGHT OF THE DAY
"NO PAIN, NO GAIN CONFERENCE!—DAY 1"

The LORD spoke to me this morning. There are so many wonderful gospel conferences that take place all over the country, and a lot of people miss out on them for one reason or another. Therefore, the LORD has used me to put together a conference! The theme for the conference this week is, "No Pain, No Gain!" Today is the first day of the conference. The LORD sent me here to let you know that all you've been dealing with, all the pain, all the hurt, all the disappointments and folks lying and back-biting on you, no matter how much it hurt, it will not compare to the glory you're going to receive from Him! That's enough to shout right there! How many of us are dealing with something? Maybe everything is hunky-dory in your life, but for the folks who have issues, for the folks who are down to their last dollar and bills are due, for the folks who are working a job and it's hell for those eight hours you're there, God is saying get ready for a miracle to take place in your life, and the miracle is going to be greater than all the pain you've ever experienced. Somebody shout, "Yeah!"

Scripture of the Day:

> For I consider that the sufferings of this present time are not worthy to be compared with the glory which shall be revealed in us.
>
> Romans 8:18 (NKJV)

Listen, you must deal with some stuff before God can elevate you. No pain, no gain! It's just that simple. For those who never have issues, I'm a bit worried about you because Christ said in this lifetime we will have trials and tribulations, but to be of good cheer! It's time to praise Him and get happy even while we're in the midst of our storms because the sufferings we're facing today will not compare to the glory that God is about to reveal to us. Can I get an *amen* for the glory you're about to receive? You've suffered long enough; it's now payback time. And remember all the pain you've experienced, God is about to give you double for your troubles! Is there anybody who wants double for their troubles? Well then, give God praise right now! Don't wait until you go to church this week to praise Him. Praise Him right now in the midst of this conference, just like you would do at the other conferences you attend. You don't leave the conference and get to your church to praise Him! You praise Him right there at the conference! No pain, no gain!

"NO PAIN, NO GAIN CONFERENCE!—DAY 2"

This is the second day of the conference, and we are dealing with how you need to give God praise in your suffering. He is setting you up for something. How many of you have delivered a child or children? Men, just follow me here. There is usually a nine month process for the pregnancy. And during these nine months, there's usually some discomfort and pain, and when the woman goes into labor there's more pain. When it's time for delivery, the pain is even stronger and the woman usually can't wait to get that child out of her. But as soon as the child is born, one of the first things the mother says is, "let me see the baby." All the pain is then forgotten because of the miracle that took place. This is very similar in the spiritual. We go through things and it's usually painful and has a lot of discomfort. The closer we get to the end of the issue, the more painful it gets. Once God brings us to the point of the breakthrough, we then look for the blessing. Because you must understand that you have to go through before the blessing comes. And if you're dealing with something right now, then you're about to go into labor! Give Him an "in spite of" praise!

Scripture of the Day:

> But may the God of all grace, who called us to His eternal glory by Christ Jesus, after you have suffered a while, perfect, establish, strengthen, and settle you.
>
> 1 Peter 5:10 (NKJV)

The key word here is after! You notice it didn't say you were perfected, established, strengthened, and settled, and *then* you suffered. It said after you suffered a while, then He settled you. Then He gave you peace. Then He strengthened you. His strength is made perfect in your weakness. Today may be the day when you go into labor. The contractions are about five to ten minutes apart, meaning folks are constantly getting on your nerves. The enemy is trying to do all he can to make you abort what God has put inside you. Don't kill the dream God gave you. Don't give in. You are too close to give up now. This is the season to get praise out and use it, because your breakthrough is right there. Matter fact, the head is out! Here comes the body. And there it is, the blessing has been birthed. Now seek it and believe it because you have to suffer for a while before your breakthrough. If you're suffering from something this morning, you are in a good place!

"NO PAIN, NO GAIN CONFERENCE!—DAY 3"

Today, we are going to focus on the fact that everything has its season. One of the issues with us as believers is that we think that just because we have now chosen to serve God, that with the click of a switch, everything should just be all right. That's not true. You have to deal with some stuff, and as long as you are in this earth suit, you will deal with issues. You will face pain and you will face sorrow in this lifetime. People are going to dislike you. Situations will arise that will try and take you out. There will be times when you will cry. You will have to deal with the fact that your loved ones will die. These are just facts of life. But do me this favor. Look in the mirror right now: the person you see has overcome poverty, debt, sorrow, pain, unemployment, health issues, people telling lies on you, etc. If you have been sustained for this long, get ready for God to bless you. If you do not endure the pain, then there will be no gain! Praise Him for keeping you thus far!

Scripture of the Day:

> To everything there is a season, A time for every purpose under heaven: A time to be born, And a time to die; A time to plant, And a time to pluck what is planted; A time to kill, And a time to heal; A time to break down, And a time to build up; A time to weep, And a time to laugh; A time to mourn, And a time to dance; A time to cast away stones, And a time to gather stones; A time to embrace, And a time to refrain from embracing; A time to gain, And a time to lose; A time to keep, And a time to throw away; A time to tear, And a time to sew; A time to keep silence, And a time to speak; A time to love, And a time to hate; A time of war, And a time of peace.
>
> Ecclesiastes 3:1–8 (NKJV)

Somewhere in there today you will be placed. Everyone will fall into one of those categories at some point in your life. God is trying to bless you, but you keep trying to avoid trouble! Let me say that again! God is trying to bless you, but you keep trying to avoid trouble! "It's good that I've been afflicted"–that's what the word says. There's a time for everything, and if you're dealing with something today, that just means that it's your time to deal with that. But you should also know that weeping may endure for a night, but joy comes in the morning! Your morning is closer than you think. Don't complain, but rejoice in your dry season because God is about to pour you out a blessing that you will not have room enough to receive–all because of the pain you've endured!

THOUGHT OF THE DAY
"NO PAIN, NO GAIN CONFERENCE!—DAY 4 THE FINALE!"

This is the last day of the No Pain, No Gain Conference! This is the day the LORD has made for us to shout. It's now time to come out of your situation. It's now time to receive what God has for you. It's now time to enter into your season that has been promised to you. No matter what the enemy has tried, no matter what your haters have tried, no weapon formed against you shall prosper. Watch this ... the weapon was formed, not to take you out, but to set you up! Somebody missed that. God allowed for the weapon to be formed in order to get you in the right position for Him to bless you. The weapon can never take you out, but it's only there to get you in the right place for God to bless you. For example, when things are going well, we don't pray as much as we need to, but as soon as something happens we go into a revival of prayer! That's because God allowed something to happen to you, only to keep you in line with the blessing He has for you. I heard a song say, "the wait is over!" That's what God is saying today! The wait is over and it's now time to receive your harvest! Is there anyone reading this that feels they are ready to receive what God has for them? If so, then praise Him right now!

Scripture of the Day:

> No weapon formed against you shall prosper, And every tongue which rises against you in judgment You shall condemn. This is the heritage of the servants of the LORD, And their righteousness is from Me,' Says the LORD.
>
> Isaiah 54:17 (NKJV)

No pain, no gain! The weapon will be formed–it just won't prosper. It won't complete the task it was sent forth to do. God will take what was meant for evil and turn it around to bless you. That's telling me that the pain will come, the suffering will come, the disappointments will come, but they will not prosper! They will not take me out. They will only position me to get that much closer to my breakthrough! Some of you are right at the brink of your breakthrough. All you need is for one more thing to try and separate you from your blessing, and if you praise God through it, your harvest will be right there for you. Don't complain today; don't get frustrated because of the attacks, just rejoice because that's a sign that you're about to have your health restored and your finances restored in the name of Jesus! Somebody shout,

"Yeah!" This may be the end of the conference, but it's the beginning of your season! I'm trying to leave it alone, but I feel something…Hallelujah!

"BEFORE YOU THOUGHT NO, GOD ALREADY SAID YES TO YOUR LIFE!"

On this day, be thankful for everything you have and everything you don't have. You could be homeless, you could be jobless, you could be without a family, you could be without food, you could be lifeless, but this is the day that the LORD has made for you. Even if you are without a job, food, or even family members and friends, you still have something more important than those things … you have life! With all that's going on around you, with all that is going on in your own life, just think that there are people who are suffering more than you are right now. Now, the question is what are you going to do about your situation? Are you going to praise the LORD until you come out of your situation, or are you going to praise your situation? Complaining and pouting about your situation is how you

praise it. One of the ways to come out is by trusting in the
LORD! You are going through what you're going through
only to strengthen you and to make sure you are truly ready
for how God is about to bless you. Just hold on to God!

Scripture of the Day:

> Before I formed you in the womb I knew you;
> Before you were born I sanctified you; I ordained
> you a prophet to the nations.
>
> Jeremiah 1:5 (NKJV)

Before your momma and daddy even held hands in
the park, before they even went on their first date, before
then … okay, you get the picture. Before all of this happened,
God already had a plan and a future of hope for you. The
blueprint of your life was already mapped out and, in the
blueprint, God placed some troubles designed to get you to
the point where He wants you to be and not where you want
to be! There is a big difference! You still have a choice. You
can follow the LORD's blueprint and receive what He has for
you, or you can do your own thing. The LORD loves you so
much that He will not force you to do anything you don't
want to do. If you choose to live your own way, then that's
what He'll allow you to do, but He will always be right there
for you when you feel in your heart you want to go to Him.
No matter what you've done in the past, He'll never turn
you way. You're hearing from a living witness. Follow what
God has for you and let Him continue to mold your life.
However, understand that there will be some bumps in the

road but know that God is with you, for He said He will never leave you, nor forsake you! Open up to Him!

THOUGHT OF THE DAY
"IT'S FOLLOWING YOU, JUST TAKE A LOOK AROUND!"

What a beautiful day this is! Let's take advantage of this day and not take it for granted. This may be the last day of work, this may be the last day of your vacation, this may be the last day of school, and this may be the last day you get to praise the Lord. If this is the last day, then let's go out praising Him! We just never know what each day may bring. Each day we wake up is a blessing because there are many people who are not waking up. Regardless of what you may be facing today, in spite of the challenges that have been placed before you, even if you may not like your job and you get frustrated knowing that you have to go in today, overlook all that and enjoy life. If you can praise the Lord for life, He will take care of your situations. He does not need any help, so stop trying to assist

God. Just give Him a praise for what He's about to do with you and rejoice and be glad in this day.

Scripture of the Day:

> Surely goodness and mercy shall follow me All the days of my life; And I will dwell in the house of the Lord Forever.
>
> Psalm 23:6 (NKJV)

Just when you thought you were forgotten; just when you thought you were going to be consumed by issues and problems; just when you thought the fight you were in had you with an eight count ... if you just take a quick peek over your shoulder, you will see that grace and mercy is right behind you. You are being followed by grace and mercy all the days of your life. No matter what is happening at this very moment in your life, take a look over your shoulder. Just think about what would happen if the twins (grace and mercy) were to take a day off. With all that is going on, we would have checked out of here a long time ago, but the Lord placed the twins there to guide us, to protect us ... God wants you to know that you are not forgotten. All that is happening or has happened was not able to destroy you. If it had destroyed you, you would not be reading this right now. Give Him praise. Stop thinking about the confusion and just let your shadows of faith take care of it. That shadow is following you. If you think you can cast a shadow when the sun is out, then know that the Son is always shinning so you will be in His light at all times. Listen. Give the Lord praise right now for whom He has placed in your life. No, not for Tyrone or Jackie or Jessie or even Troy, but grace and mercy!

"DO YOU HAVE A PLAN, BECAUSE THE ENEMY DOES!"

Often, we forget why Christ ever came to earth, but we always remember why the enemy comes. There's so much going on in our lives that we tend to accept anything. For example, you've been in debt so long that you have now just accepted it. You've been in that neighborhood so long that you've now accepted that you will never be elevated from there. You've been unemployed so long that you feel that you need to stop sending your resumes. But Christ has come to give us a more abundant life, and that's a promise He made. If He does not come through with His promise then that makes Him a liar and He can't lie! What we need to do is ask ourselves a question. What am I doing to get out of what I'm in? I'll let you think about that for a minute and then I'll move on …

Scripture of the Day:

The thief does not come except to steal, and to kill, and to destroy. I have come that they may have life, and that they may have it more abundantly.

John 10:10 (NKJV)

Read that again please. Okay, now read it again. Notice that the thief has a purpose. He has a plan. Watch this ... he has a vision! And it's to steal, kill, and destroy us. Why does the enemy have a purpose, a plan, and a vision, but we don't? Without a vision, the people perish. This is why you're dealing with what you're dealing with longer than what God expected–because you have no vision. You don't see your way out of what you're going through. If you're having trouble with your finances, then make a plan on how to save money and pay your debt off, but don't keep spending, knowing you don't have it like that! Christ came not only to give us life, but He came to give us a more abundant life, meaning He wants us to live in prosperity. He wants us to be healthy. He wants us to have joy and peace, but if you cannot understand that you need a vision, then you will continue to be broke! It's really very simple. The enemy has been exposed. The Scripture tells us why He has come, but it then tells us why Christ came. You must decide whom you will follow.

"TAKE A RISK WITH YOUR NOW FAITH!"

Are you ready to achieve every goal you've set for yourself? Are you ready for the next level in Christ? Here's the key to getting there and it's very simple. You must have faith! Here's what God is looking for in this season. First, let me say this, this season is open and there's a harvest for those who want to receive. The flood gates are open and this is the time where God is pouring out a supernatural blessing and it has your name on it. This is why the enemy is attacking you so much. This is why you feel as if you want to go back into the world and go to the club and smoke and drink. The enemy has caught a glimpse of where God wants to bring you, but your faith hasn't caught up with the miracle. There's no need to blame God. There's no need to blame society. There's no need to blame your job, because God is not concerned with that. He's only concerned with the place

He wants to bring you! But it's your lack of faith that's causing you to miss the mark. Okay, now let me tell you what God is looking for today. He's looking for some risk takers! Let me share the scripture and I'll come back to that.

Scripture of the Day:

> Now faith is the substance of things hoped for, the evidence of things not seen.
>
> Hebrews 11:1 (NKJV)

What type of faith is God looking for? Now faith! Not yesterday's faith. Not last week's faith. Not last year's faith. Not the faith you had when you first got saved. God wants some now faith. He wants some risk-taking faith. Take a risk and start that business. Take a risk and go back to school. Take a risk and go into full-time ministry. Take a risk and plant seeds. Take a risk and pay more than 10 percent in tithes. When you take a risk, you will receive all the things that were not seen. You will receive everything you hoped for! But it's going to start with your now faith! Today I want you to do something different. Don't engage in just the same old Monday routine. Today take a risk and trust God. Whatever it is He put on your heart sometime ago, take a risk and do it today!

THOUGHT OF THE DAY
"HE BROUGHT ME THIS FAR FOR A REASON!"

I have instructions from the LORD that are a bit different today. I want you to pray! Anoint your house. Go to work and anoint your work place. Anoint your desk or your cubicle. Anoint your children. Anoint your family members. Watch this, anoint your checkbook! Anoint yourself. Pray for those unsaved family members. Pray for our children. Pray for those in Iraq. Pray for your neighbors. Pray for your community. Pray for healing in your body. Pray for teachers. Pray for the schools. Pray for those in college. Pray for those in ministry. Pray for pastors. Pray for bishops. Pray for the glory of the LORD to take over the earth. Pray for unity amongst Christians. Pray for sinners. Pray for lawyers. Pray for doctors. Pray for your business to prosper. Pray for your practice to prosper. Pray your way out of debt. Pray your way into a miracle. Pray for peace. Pray for those incarcerated. Pray for the youth! Pray for the homeless. Pray for single mothers. Pray for single fathers. Pray for grace! Pray for His mercy!

Worship the LORD today! Worship the LORD today! Everything you've prayed for shall come to pass, but it's going to hurt first! But thus sayeth the LORD, I heard your prayer and help is on the way. It's already done! Pray! Pray! Pray! God sat me down to type this to someone who was about to give up on life; someone who was about to give up on their business; someone who was about to give up on God. Pray! The devil is a liar! Pray! Pray! Pray! Your miracle is on its way. You've suffered for a while and according to 1 Peter 5:10, now God is going to strengthen you, establish you and perfect you in His strength! Keep praying! You're almost there! He's worthy! He's worthy to be praised! I'm trying to stop, but I feel the presence of the LORD! Pray! Pray for your newborn child that God will use them in a mighty way! Pray for that child that has not been born yet! Pregnant women right now, in the name of Jesus, anoint your stomachs. Pray! Now praise Him for what's taking place today. I know you're at work and people are watching you, but God has a miracle for you. Who cares if they are watching? You know what you need from God. Praise Him!

THOUGHT OF THE DAY
"LEARN!"

This may not be one of those shouting messages, but just hold on before you hit delete because it's still a word from the LORD! In the church, we have come to a point where we just want to be preached to. And don't get me wrong, that's wonderful, but we also need to be taught. There is a difference between preaching and teaching. If a preacher comes in and teaches on fornication, back-biting, gossiping, etc, we don't want to hear it, so we may either fall asleep or just get up and leave. Now if the same preacher comes in and talks about how you're that close to your breakthrough, all of a sudden we say we are hearing from the LORD. We have to stop that! Also, the preacher may come in and teach on how to become rich. Again, we don't want to hear that because we want the riches without the issues. I heard Biggie Smalls say, "Mo-money, Mo-problems!" It's time to start learning the word of God and the principles that come with it and stop wanting everything to fall out of the sky for us. We must keep an open mind to learn!

Scripture of the Day:

> My people are destroyed for lack of knowledge. Because you have rejected knowledge, I also will reject you from being priest for Me; Because you have forgotten the law of your God, I also will forget your children.
>
> Hosea 4:6 (NKJV)

Ouch! Not only will you be forgotten, but God says He will also forget your children if you choose not to learn the law of your God, which will give you knowledge. Many people are being destroyed today because they lack knowledge. They've gotten to a point where they feel no one can teach them anything. You know those people in the church that have been there for up-teen years and now, because the pastor may be younger than them, they feel like they can't be taught. What they don't understand is that they are slowly perishing because they refuse to learn. Also, the generation under them will be forgotten by the LORD because of their lack of knowledge. Let's learn something new everyday for the rest of our lives. Also, read more of the Bible!

THOUGHT OF THE DAY
"WHO ARE YOU
CALLING ON TODAY?"

Let me ask this question and it may be silly. How many of you reading this today either feel like giving up or you are just dealing with some issues that are truly a burden to you right now? Raise your right hand if this is you. I'll close my eyes so I can't see who raises their hand. Personally, if I had three hands, all of them would be raised. You have just gotten past the first step of being delivered. The first step to being delivered is admitting you have an issue. Now I want to ask, why have you been depending and calling on man to assist you? That's what the LORD told me to ask some of you. You've gotten to a point that you've been in your situation for so long that you've felt as if God has forgotten you or that He has not heard your prayers, and because of that, you have now put your total dependence on man. You have now focused on man to get you out of the situation that's been hindering you. But God sent this word this morning to let you know that you need to call on Him and Him only! And as a result of calling on Him here's what will take place … (in case of emergency read below).

Scripture of the Day:

> Call to Me, and I will answer you, and show you
> great and mighty things, which you do not know.
> Jeremiah 33:3 (NKJV)

Call to whom? God said, "Call to me!" And not only will He come to your aid when you call on Him, but He said when He answers you He's going to show you great things which your mind couldn't even imagine. God wants to bless you in a manner that you will be blown away, but you have to call on Him! Now understand, He may not come when you want Him to, but He's always on time. And just the fact that you call on His name makes the demons shake. Even if you don't feel God has heard you when you call His name, the demons in hell heard you call His name, and every time you call on Him, He will slap every devil that's messing with you. That's why you don't feel God is there with you when you call on Him, because He's fighting your battles when you call on Him. He's transferring money into your bank account when you call on Him. He's changing the doctor's report when you call on Him. He's going to show you great and mighty things. All you have to do is call on Him and then believe it's done! Praise Him right now!

THOUGHT OF THE DAY
"CAN I KEEP IT REAL TODAY?"

Let's start today off by just keeping it real. There will be no scripture today, just something to think about as you go through your day. I was coming from the store last night and there was a lot of traffic, and as I got closer to what took place, all I could do was pray. I saw the aftermath of a horrific car accident. I mean, it looked as if two cars hit head on. The cars were the size of one car because the front of each car was pushed in so much. All of a sudden, here's what hit me. We go through our day and we complain about so much. We worry about bills and we stress over our job and sometimes we even think about giving up. Just think for a quick moment, what if that was you in that car accident?

I know today is a bit different, but here's what God gave me last night. As the individuals were clinging to their lives, do you think they were thinking about how their bills were going to get paid? Do you think they were thinking about their jobs? Or do you think they were thinking about giving up on a certain situation in their life? Here's what else was interesting to me. All the traffic drove by the accident! What are you saying? What I'm saying is even with this horrific incident that took place, life still goes on! My point is, if you feel like giving up, life will still go on! If you feel like you're not going to make it through, life will still go on! Even if you feel like suicide is the answer–not to sound harsh, but just keeping it real–life will still go on! Because have you noticed at funerals, that once it's over, you leave, and then eventually, you have to go back to work? I know it was painful, but you still needed to do what you needed to do to live! Beginning today, let's be more appreciative that we have life and let's do like Psalms 150: because you have breath, praise the LORD!

THOUGHT OF THE DAY
"IT'S ALREADY DONE!"

Listen, let me just get right into it this morning. You have already been called out. You have already been chosen. The enemy can't do a thing to you unless you allow it to happen. The only one who can stop your miracle is you! You were ordained to be a prophet over the nations. It's time to start believing the report of the LORD and not the report of the world. I know you're dealing with some stuff right now. I know there are issues up the creek in your life. I know bills have you pulling your hair out. But God does not call those who will fail, and because you have been called out, you have victory. In spite of what the situation looks like right now, you still have victory. Folks have lied on you, they have set traps on you, they have spread untrue gossip about you, but you are still called. You have to walk on your promise and not what you currently see. That's why we walk by faith and not by sight; because what we see right now is not the finished product, but only part of the process to get us to the finished product, which is our blessing! Just shake off whatever you're dealing with today and move on in life!

Scripture of the Day:

> Before I formed you in the womb I knew you;
> Before you were born I sanctified you; I ordained
> you a prophet to the nations.
>
> Jeremiah 1:5 (NKJV)

Before your momma and daddy went on their first date, God was already putting the blueprint together for your life. It says before you were formed, God already knew you. Before you were born, God already sanctified you. This means He was setting you apart. He set you apart from depression. He set you apart from destruction. He set you apart from sickness. Even though these things may come into your life, you truly have already defeated them in the name of Jesus! God wants us to have the best and He wants us to live our lives to the fullest. So, there is no need for depression. There is no need for stress. There is no need for doubts. Just trust in the LORD and every time negative thoughts creep into your head, remind the LORD that you are called! Get ready for your miracle and remember- no matter what the situation looks like, the miracle has already been formed! Just receive it!

THOUGHT OF THE DAY
"CAN WE JUST
TALK TODAY?"

Today is different. There are two things the LORD put on my heart this morning to share with you. There will be no scripture today. God told me that there are two things needed for your breakthrough. First, you need to repent! Yeah, I know you may say you haven't done anything, but then maybe this isn't for you. But for all those who made mistakes and for all those who truly want to come out of the mess they're in and for all those who know they are that close to their season, then God said to repent this morning.

Second, God said to seek Him for the next decision you're about to make. Many of you have a difficult decision to make and you're about to make that decision based on the flesh. Meaning, because you don't see a way out, you just want to give up; because you don't see the harvest of that business and you've been planting seeds into it, you want

to give it up. You've been alone for so long and this man/
woman has been treating you so nice, but because you're a
Christian you're hesitant about the next step because he/she
is trying to pressure you into something you know is wrong.
God is saying, "Seek Me first!"

Thought of the Next Minute:

Repent and seek God for guidance on your next
decision!

"EVERY TIME
I TURN AROUND ...
JESUS, JESUS!"

You all may have heard the song before, "Every time I turn around ... Bling, Bling" by the No Limit Soldiers. Well today, it's every time I turn around, Jesus, Jesus! Not now! I'm saying that to the person who is at the point of their breakthrough but feel as if God has forgotten about them. Not now! For that person who has bills and the money isn't coming in like it used to and you want to give up on the business you started. The strength of the LORD is here, and if you give in now, you will miss the opportunity of your breakthrough. You're probably saying, "Well, Troy, you don't understand what I'm going through." That may be true, but I do understand that when you're down to nothing that means God is up to something. The promises of the LORD are on the way. Just a little while longer is what God is saying this morning. And know this, Romans 8:18 says that the sufferings of this present time will not compare to the glory you are about to receive. That means no matter what you're going through right now, God has a blessing in store for you that will be greater than all the pain you've endured. Just start praising Him right now!

Scripture of the Day:

> Have I not commanded you? Be strong and of good courage; do not be afraid, nor be dismayed, for the LORD your God is with you wherever you go.
>
> Joshua 1:9 (NKJV)

No matter where you go, God is right there with you. He's with you in the courthouse. He's with you in the hospital. He's with you at your job. He's with you when folks disappoint you. He's with you when the haters hate on you. God said He would never leave you, nor forsake you. And because He's always there, you need to be strong and of good courage and start believing that your miracle is right around the corner. Let the devil know that, "I ain't neva scar'd!" The glory of the LORD is about to come into your life and everything that seemed out of order is now about to take its rightful place and get in order. Just keep looking towards the hills from which comes thy help. Praise Him right now for He is with you!

THOUGHT OF THE DAY
"WHEN I MOVE, YOU MOVE ... JUST LIKE THAT!"

When you go to a restaurant, the waiter usually comes to take your order. You tell him/her what you want and they bring you exactly what you want or you ask them to bring your food back until they get the order right. If they didn't want to serve you, they wouldn't say to you, "May I take your order please?" Understand that once an order is made, it has to be fulfilled. Today I hear the Spirit saying to us, "When I move, you move ... just like that!" God has given us the order and now we must fulfill the order. Since the order is given, even if we mess up it doesn't mean that God will cast us out. That's why we need to thank God for grace! We serve a forgiving God, and all you have to do is come to Him with a sincere heart, asking for forgiveness when you make a mistake. But even in the midst of your mistakes, your steps are still ordered by the LORD! I just want you to follow the Holy Spirit today because He is saying to us, "When I move, you move...just like that!"

Scripture of the Day:

> The steps of a good man are ordered by the LORD, And He delights in his way. Though he fall, he shall not be utterly cast down; For the LORD upholds him with His hand.
>
> Psalm 37:23–24 (NKJV)

Verse 24 really sums it up. This verse indicates that even if you fall, you will not be cast down because the LORD upholds you with His hand. Even if people give up on you because you failed at something, God hasn't given up on you. Even when people reject you, God won't reject you. Even when folks judge you because of your mistakes, God forgives because your steps have been ordered. What we must understand is that even the ordered steps come with mistakes. Somebody missed that! God knows we can't be sinless. He just wants us to sin less! But thank God for the order. Our steps are ordered and they are not ordered by that controlling boyfriend/girlfriend. They are not ordered by that nagging spouse. They are not ordered by that complaining Christian from your church. Rather, your steps are ordered by the LORD. When I move, you move...just like that!

THOUGHT OF THE DAY
"LOVE, SO MANY PEOPLE USE YOUR NAME IN VAIN!"

Today, let's share with someone else the greatest gift of all: love! In these last and evil days, there is one thing we are lacking the most, and that's love. We need to start acting like we love one another instead of just saying it. Our love, which we say we have for one another, often only lasts for a quick minute. For example, at church the preacher gets up and before he/she preaches, they ask if everyone could look around them and give someone a hug and tell them you love them. The atmosphere is great for that quick moment. All you hear is folks saying how much they love one another and people going out of their way to hug each other. But then something happens ... as soon as church is over, all you have to do is accidentally cut someone off in the parking lot and that same person who walked all the way from their row to hug you and tell you how much they love you is now cussing you out! Today we're talking about Love! Love with a capital "L" and not a lowercase "l." It's time to forgive one another and move on. It is time to show one another Love and not love! Love with the lowercase "l" is the type that will smile at you one moment and talk about you the next!

Scripture of the Day:

Love suffers long and is kind; love does not envy; love does not parade itself, is not puffed up; does not have behave rudely, does not seek its own, is not provoked, thinks no evil; does not rejoice in iniquity, but rejoices in truth; bears all things, believes all things, hopes all things, endure all things. Love never fails. But whether there are prophecies, they will fail; whether there are tongues, they will cease; whether there is knowledge, it will vanish away. For we know in part and we prophesy in part. But when that which is perfect has come, then that which is in part will be done away. When I was a child, I spoke as a child, I understood as a child, I thought as a child; but when I became a man, I put away childish things. For now we see in a mirror, dimly, but then face to face. Now I know in part, but then I shall know just as I also am known. And now abide faith, hope, love, these three; but the greatest of these is love.

1 Corinthians 13:4–13 (NKJV)

Need I say more?

"VICTORY TOLD ME TO SAY HI TO YOU TODAY, BECAUSE IT'S HERE!"

This morning, God showed me the strategy to getting victory over every situation we face in life. Do you want to know how to get victory over everything you encounter in life? Do you really want to know? Okay, here it is. It's really very simple. Just show up! I'll say it again because somebody missed it. Just show up! We just had the Olympics and as a basketball fan, I was a little disappointed in the men because they were expected to win the gold medal, but they only won the bronze medal. They were there, but they didn't show up. What do you mean? If you watched any of the games, you would have noticed that they didn't even play like themselves. It was almost as if they thought they would go over there and it would be easy for them, but then the situation got very intense. However, by the time they noticed, it was too late. The same thing happens to us. We have issues and circumstances in our lives and we face these things, but we don't show up for them. We face our issues, but we don't have praise in the midst of our issues. We face our storms, but we decide to stay home from church because of the storm we're in. We face our problems, but instead of praying our way out, we try to find a man to get us out. We're facing our situations, but we're not showing up for them. Showing up means you have praise with you in spite of what it looks like. Showing up means even when there's no way out, you still stand up and say, "He'll make a way out of no way." All you have to do today is show up and God will do the rest!

Scripture of the Day:

> But thanks be to God, who gives us the victory
> through our LORD Jesus Christ.
>
> 1 Corinthians 15:57 (NKJV)

Read that again! Read it one more time! Thanks is praise. That's why the scripture says, "Thanks be to God!" And it says that first. It's at the beginning of the sentence. We need to just start a praise right now because the victory over that situation you're facing has already been given. Tell your bills you have victory over them. Tell your job you have victory over it. Tell that sickness you have victory over it. Tell those haters and gossipers you have victory over them. Tell depression you have victory over it. In the name of Jesus, it's time to just start praising Him because the battle is not yours–it belongs to the LORD. And because He has already defeated the enemy and all his tricks and schemes, all we have to do today is show up and receive what God has for us. Don't look at your current situation, but seek the finish line! I believe that if somebody shouts, "I got victory," you will start the process of coming out of whatever it was that had you bound. Just show up!

THOUGHT OF THE DAY
"THERE'S NOTHING WRONG WITH BEING ABSENT!"

As the rapper Mase said, "Welcome back!" The Lord put this on my heart to share with you all regarding death. This may not be a shouting message today, but it's still a word from the Lord! How many of us have lost a loved one who we know was saved? God told me to tell you that they are all right. Now the key word is "saved!" If you are not saved when your time comes, then you will not be all right. But for those who have lost a loved one, whether it was last week, last year, five years ago, or ten years ago, God told me to let you know that they are all right. Once they pass on and they get into heaven, they actually become cheerleaders for us who are still here. They want to make sure that we live right and that we get to know the Lord on a personal basis before the death angel comes, so that they might see us again. We often say that they are absent, but actually, it is us who are absent! I know you have goals in life and there's nothing wrong with that, but your ultimate goal should be that you spend your life in eternity with the LORD! And if you want to live here permanently, then you are absent!

Scripture of the Day:

> We are confident, yes, well pleased rather to be absent from the body and to be present with the LORD.
>
> 2 Corinthians 5:8 (NKJV)

Once you get to know the LORD on a personal basis and make Him your LORD and Savior, the Bible says that you will become confident and pleased to know that you would rather be absent from this body, absent from this flesh, and absent from all the hell we encounter here on earth, in order to be present with the LORD! God sent me here to encourage you this morning. All of those family members and friends that passed away that you loved, they are all right as long as they knew Christ as their personal Savior. They are absent from this body, but they are in the very presence of the LORD! I know it's tough and it's okay to cry and have moments, but don't allow your sorrow to become permanent. Your loved ones are not crying. They are cheering. And all they want is for us to get it right so that one day we can be present with the LORD!

THOUGHT OF THE DAY
"P.U.S.H.!"

P.U.S.H.! **Praise Until Something Happens!** I'm piggy-backing off of yesterday's word. The LORD told me that this is not the season to give up. Now let me tell you what you need to bring to the table when your season hits. The LORD did say, "[He will] prepare a table before me in the presence of my enemies" (Psalm 23:5 NKJV). That means that once the table is complete, it's time for your season. All you need to bring with you to receive your breakthrough is praise! That's it! Listen, it's time to praise our way out. Shout our way out. P.U.S.H.! Praise Until Something Happens! God is looking for some people who don't mind shouting in front of folks. He's looking for some people who will shout even when the camera is not on them in church. He's looking for some people who will shout at work, who will shout at a business meeting, who will shout in the grocery store. It's not the season to try and be cute. You know what you need from God, so you might as well start praising Him right now! Is there anyone reading this that needs a miracle today? Well P.U.S.H.!

Scripture of the Day:

> I will bless the LORD at all times; His praise shall continually be in my mouth. My soul shall make its boast in the LORD; The humble shall hear of it and be glad. Oh, magnify the LORD with me, And let us exalt His name together.
>
> Psalm 34:1–3 (NKJV)

God is saying, P.U.S.H! The blessing is right there, but you have to P.U.S.H! The miracle is right there, but you have to P.U.S.H! Praise Until Something Happens! Don't give up now. Give Him a crazy praise because He's about to give you a crazy blessing. Folks' mouths are going to drop when they see you praising Him like you're crazy. But when God brings you out, they'll understand why you were acting like that. Forget about who's watching. You said you needed a miracle. If you truly need a miracle, then God said bring praise to the table because your season is right in place. Bless the LORD at all times! You need to keep praise on you like identification or like American Express; don't ever leave home without it! P.U.S.H! Even while you're dealing with that divorce, P.U.S.H! Even while you're dealing with being a single parent, P.U.S.H! Even with you dealing with being unemployed right now, P.U.S.H! Even with your ministry at a standstill, P.U.S.H! God is up to something. All you need to do to receive what He has for you is keep praising! Praise Until Something Happens!

"LET'S MOVE AHEAD!"

God spoke to me this morning as I was getting up to share this word with you. It's time to stop living in the past. Yes, you made mistakes and they still hurt sometimes, but God is saying that it's now time to live and to live abundantly. This is going to sound crazy, but listen... God is not concerned with your past. He's not concerned with that divorce you went through eight years ago. He's not concerned with the drugs you used back in the day. He's not concerned that you were abused as a child. He's not concerned that you were sexually assaulted. He's not concerned that you filed for bankruptcy two years ago. God is more concerned with your future! All that stuff is in the past and it doesn't mean that He doesn't care about the things that hurt you, but what He's saying is that He has prepared a place for you in the future, a future of hope. But if you continue to allow your past to hinder you, then that's your fault. Watch this. Pay close attention to this. Isn't it funny that those who did those trifling things to you in the past are not concerned? They are living their lives. Why don't we go ahead and live our lives. Stop making excuses because God already set your future in place. Just go and get it.

Scripture of the Day:

> For I know the thoughts that I think toward you, says the LORD, thoughts of peace and not of evil, to give you a future of hope. Then you will call upon Me and go and pray to Me, and I will listen to you.
>
> Jeremiah 29:11–12 (NKJV)

This is the LORD speaking. He already knows your future and it is a future of hope. Your future has peace. Then He says call on Him in prayer and He will listen. If you feel God is not hearing your prayers you need to check who you're praying to! Understand that God wants you prosperous. He wants you healthy. He wants you out of debt. However, it doesn't mean you're not going to deal with some stuff along the journey. It's the future God is more concerned about. If you're living in the past, then you are missing the mark. And when you miss the mark, you miss out on what God has for you. Shake it off this morning and move forward and stop hitting the rewind button on your life!

THOUGHT OF THE DAY
"GO GET'EM!"

It's time to go and get those who are lost! I don't care if they live in a $200,000 home or if they drive a Lexus or if they are the CEO of a company. If they don't know the LORD Jesus on a personal basis and have a personal relationship with Him, then they are lost. All of the lost are not poor or live in a one-bedroom apartment or are on local state assistance programs. Some of them are, but all of them are not. We have to go and get our family members who are not saved. We have to go and get our coworkers who are not saved. We have to go and get that person who you work out with at the gym who is not saved. Watch this ... we even have to get that person who goes to church only because they feel it's the right thing to do but they are not saved. We have to share the good news of Jesus to all the nations. Here's one problem in the church today. Many churches have a core membership that is enough to pay the bills, pay the pastor's salary, and enough to allow the church to function financially. But because of this, no one is witnessing anymore! (Oops!) The devil is a liar! Go and tell someone how God has been good to you. Stop being selfish.

Scripture of the Day:

> 'Go therefore and make disciples of all the nations, baptizing them in the name of the Father and of the Son and of the Holy Spirit, teaching them to observe all things that I have commanded you; and lo, I am with you always, even to the end of the age.'
>
> Matthew 28:19–20 (NKJV)

Do you see the key word in these scriptures? Of course Father, Son, and Holy Spirit are key words, but there is another key word. I'll give you a minute to look for it. Okay, time's up. The other key word there is, "Go!" I did a study, this is Troyology! I discovered that many people are not going to give their lives to the LORD by reading the Bible first. They'll read the Bible after they give their lives to the LORD! But many people are going to give their lives to the LORD according to the person who has witnessed to them. You have to make sure you're on fire for the LORD when you witness to them and you have to go out to get them. It's fine to pray folk will come to church, but the Bible says faith without works is dead. That means you can have all the faith in the world, but if you're not putting it to work then you will not see any results. Today, share the word of God with someone. Also, we have to stop preaching to folks who are already saved. Don't get me wrong, I know they need a word of encouragement. However, my point is while ministering to the saved, don't forget about those who don't know Him!

THOUGHT OF THE DAY
"INCREASE!"

Today, I want you all to follow along. It's going to be a bit different. Let me first ask you this question: are you ready for increase? Don't fool with me. Are you really ready for increase? Ok, then read the scriptures below ... and be blessed!

Scripture of the Day:

> May the LORD give you increase more and more,
> You and your children.
>
> Psalm 115:14 (NKJV)

> May the LORD give you increase more and more,
> You and your children.
>
> Psalm 115:14 (NKJV)

May the LORD give you increase more and more,
You and your children.

Psalm 115:14 (NKJV)

May the LORD give you increase more and more,
You and your children.

Psalm 115:14 (NKJV)

May the LORD give you increase more and more,
You and your children.

Psalm 115:14 (NKJV)

May the LORD give you increase more and more,
You and your children.

Psalm 115:14 (NKJV)

May the LORD give you increase more and more,
You and your children.

Psalm 115:14 (NKJV)

This scripture is repeated seven times! The number seven means completion! Get this down in your spirit. We had a gentlemen speak at the church yesterday who used to quote this scripture ten times a day for forty days! Somebody needs to praise God right now for increase! I told you it was different today, but the results are the same: Victory!

"DO YOU HAVE A HOLE IN YOUR POCKET?"

You're probably saying, "What type of question is that?" Well, here's what I mean. Have you ever experienced a time where you paid off a bill and then you thought you had extra money. But all of a sudden something else happened, and the money you were trying to save had to be used for another unexpected situation in your life? You'll have about three more car payments to go before that car is yours, and as soon as you pay the car off, it breaks down and now you need a new car! If similar situations like this happen in your life, it means you have a hole in your pocket. Every time you get ready to save money, something happens. Now let me ask you this question: Are you paying your tithes and offerings? This is the command God has put over our life to pay Him 10 percent of your gross pay; not the net pay of your paycheck, but the gross. That means if you're paying 9.999

percent, you're missing the mark. For example, if you make $1,000 a week, God wants $100! Understand that God can make the $900 go farther than that $1,000 if you obey Him by paying your tithes! Today I want you to be honest with yourself and ask yourself this question, "Am I truly paying my tithes and offerings?" The answer you give will determine if you have a hole in your pocket.

Scripture of the Day:

> Will a man rob God? Yet you have robbed Me!
> But you say, 'In what way have we robbed You?'
> In tithes and offerings.
>
> Malachi 3:8 (NKJV)

Please do not be offended by me. But if you're not paying your tithes and offerings, you are a thief! I may not get a whole lot of amen's or responses back, but I have to be obedient. The LORD spoke to me about this just as I sat down. He doesn't care how much you shout. He doesn't care how much you run around the church. He doesn't even care if you preached a good message. If you're not paying Him what He has commanded, then you're missing the mark. And when you miss the mark, you will have a whole in your pocket. Just stop screaming, running, crying with snot running out your nose, and shouting how much you love God if you're not obeying Him with the tithes. Just stop it. I'm not saying that in judgment. I'm saying it because you may be fooling your pastor but you're not fooling God! We are in this together and I want all my brothers and sisters in Christ to prosper. Let's be real with ourselves and with God and rewrite that check for Sunday. This time make it out for the entire 10 percent!

THOUGHT OF THE DAY
"YOU BETTER TAKE YO MOUTH OFF ME!"

This is truly the day the LORD has made. You need to stop reading this and rejoice and be glad that you are in it. Today's topic is something that doesn't discriminate. It's happening everywhere–in every neighborhood, in every job, in every church. In fact, as long as there are people on this earth we will have this issue. It's gossip! Why do people gossip? I have the answer. The answer is people gossip and talk about folks to take the spotlight off of themselves! They talk about Sister Such-&-Such and they lie on her and say she's cheating on her husband only because that's what they are doing. Men accuse the ladies of doing this all the time because we do it too! Men gossip just as much. They talk about Brother Such-&-Such getting elevated to a new position only because they thought the position was designed for them! For all the gossipers and back-biters and liars, the same measure you use with your mouths on other folk, guess what … it's coming back to you! You need to be careful who you put your mouth on today!

Scripture of the Day:

> He who leads into captivity shall go into captivity; he who kills with the sword must be killed with the sword. Here is the patience and the faith of the saints.
>
> Revelations 13:10 (NKJV)

Now what I mean by putting your mouth on someone is not kissing them, but talking about them. If you lead someone into captivity, for example by lying and scheming so someone can be bound up, then the same measure will come back to you. And when it comes back to you, it's going to be more intense then what you did to the person. If you kill with the sword, meaning if you kill someone with your mouth by slandering them, then it's coming back to you. In the book of Isaiah it says, "No weapon formed against me shall prosper." The "B" part of that scripture says any tongue that rises up against me, God shall condemn. If you want to keep talking about me, go ahead, but know that God is going to judge you for it. When the haters talk about you and gossip, just keep doing what you're doing because they only do that when you're doing good! If you were not doing anything of significance, then they wouldn't talk. Don't retaliate; just praise God because He got yo back and yo front! Today, please be aware that before you talk about someone, whatever you say will come back to you!

THOUGHT OF THE DAY
"HE LOVES ME, HE LOVES ME NOT ... "

This is going to sound like a crazy question. You'll probably say, "Now, what kind of question is that?" You ready? Okay, here we go. Who wants to be blessed by God? Before you answer that question, take a minute and think about this. Do you love Christ for who He is, or do you love Christ for what He does? Christ is going to put you to the test. Why? Because you did say that you wanted to be blessed today, right? That was you. Christ is going to ask you this question, "Do you love Me?" This is not a trick question but please think about this before you just shout out yes! If you love Christ, the world will hate you. If you follow Christ, the enemy will never stop trying to take you out. If you follow Christ, He is going to ask the question, "Do you love Me?" After Christ asks you this question, He's then going to command you to serve in one way or another. He's testing you to see where you really are with Him. Do you just love Him for His miracles, or do you love Him for who He is? Are you sure you're willing to carry out the things He commands you to do? Things that make you go hmm!

Scripture of the Day:

> So when they had eaten breakfast, Jesus said to Simon Peter, 'Simon, son of Jonah, do you love Me more than these?' He said to Him, 'Yes, LORD; You know that I love You.' He said to him, 'Feed My lambs.' He said to him again a second time, 'Simon, son of Jonah, do you love Me?' He said to Him, 'Yes, LORD; You know that I love You.' He said to him, 'Tend My sheep.' He said to him the third time, 'Simon, son of Jonah, do you love Me?' Peter was grieved because He said to him the third time, 'Do you love Me?' And he said to Him, 'LORD, You know all things; You know that I love You.' Jesus said to Him, 'Feed My sheep.'
>
> John 21:15–17 (NKJV)

Christ wants to really make sure that you love Him, so He's going to ask you more than once because He knows that by the third time, many of us will become aggravated and will probably deny who He is. Before you receive that breakthrough you've been praying for, before that healing comes you've been fasting for, before that miracle takes place in your home or work or church, Christ is going to ask you this question: "Do you love Me?" And then He's going to ask you a second time and then a third time. If you are one of those who get frustrated when asked the same question more than once, then you may not want to even consider asking the LORD for a blessing today because one of the requirements to receiving the blessing is you must love Christ and be willing to serve Him. If you have a problem doing any one of those things, then don't bother asking to be blessed. And don't think you can just say you love Him and that's it. He's going to put you to the test to make sure you're sincere with what you say. He loves me, He loves me not!

THOUGHT OF THE DAY
"CHECK THE CLIQUE YOU ROLL WITH!"

Last night was a strange night. I had several dreams and they were all different, but had the same moral at the end of each story. The moral was to "Check the clique you roll wit'!" I shared this with someone at my church yesterday. I pray you receive it. When a woman is pregnant, the baby receives food through what she eats. The only way the baby can eat is when the momma eats. The food is received not through the baby's mouth, but through the umbilical cord. The baby depends on the momma to feed him/her. The baby can't do it on its own. But after the nine month process, when the baby is born, the first thing the doctors do is cut the umbilical cord. The baby cries because he/she is out on their own and now they have to learn to feed on their own. Here's where I'm going with this. There are some people around you, some folks you hang out with at the job, even some people from the church, that all they do is feed off you! They share in your gifts. They share your anointing. They are literally hindering you from where God is trying to bring you. And it's because you're feeding them through your spiritual unbiblical cord. What you need to do today is cut the cord! In other words, cut some people from your circle of friends. Let them go out on their own because God is ready to perform a miracle in your life and you don't need people clinging onto you holding you back! Check the clique you roll wit'!

Scripture of the Day:

A man who has friends must himself be friendly, But there is a friend who sticks closer than a brother.

Proverbs 18:24 (NKJV)

First of all, if you don't have any true friends, you must first show yourself to be friendly. But I want you today to focus on the B part of that scripture. "But there is a friend who sticks closer than a brother." You see, just because you talk with them, just because you eat lunch together, just because you shared something with them and maybe this time they didn't spread your business, just because they loaned you money, that doesn't mean they are your friend! If they were a true friend, when they loaned you money the whole department at your job wouldn't know about it. You need to pray to the LORD and ask the LORD to send you people who will stick closer than a brother. There are some out there, but you haven't really experienced them yet because you're allowing your flesh to pick your friends instead of the Holy Spirit! You don't have time to keep getting disappointed. God is trying to bless you, but you keep putting these so-called friends ahead of God! And God is such a gentleman that He will not force Himself on you. He'll just allow you to stay in that mess until you finally come to Him for answers and not your girlfriend or boyfriend! It's time to check the clique you roll wit'! By the end of the day, you should have removed some folks from your list! The Holy Spirit just shared with me as I was about to close to say this. You know who the people are who need to be removed, but you are afraid to remove them because they have something on you! Either some gossip, some dirt, your past … something! But God said to tell you to remove them right now, in Jesus' name!

"IT'S COMING (7) TIMES HARDER THIS TIME!"

want you to take a look in the mirror this morning. Now, what do you see? I ask that question because I want to make sure that you know you! Here's how the enemy is having so much success with us today: because we don't know ourselves. What do you mean? What I mean is if you know you have an alcohol problem, why are you continuing to go to happy hour with the folks from your job? If you know you have a lust issue, why do you keep going to Hooters to have lunch? (Oops!) Understand this, whatever you've been delivered from, it's coming back! And this time, when it comes back, it's bringing seven of his friends with it. That means it's coming back seven times as strong. That's why you have people who've quit smoking for the tenth time. When they initially decided to quit, the urge came back stronger each time they quit. The enemy has something that most of us don't have and that's patience! The enemy will wait for the right time to attack. He tried to take you out in 1999 and he failed, but he didn't give up. He tried to take you out in 2001 and he failed, but he didn't give up. He was being patient and the next time he comes, he's bringing seven friends with him!

Scripture of the Day:

> When an unclean spirit goes out of a man, he goes through dry places, seeking rest, and finds none. Then he says, 'I will return to my house from which I came.' And when he comes, he finds it empty, swept, and put in order. Then he goes and takes with him **seven** other spirits more wicked than himself, and they enter and dwell there; and the last state of that man is worse than the first. So shall it also be with this wicked generation.
>
> Matthew 12:43–45 (NKJV)

Did you read that? I mean, did you really read that until it got into your spirit? Those old habits are creeping back and this time they're stronger than ever before. This is why we have to make sure we know who we are and whose we are! Make sure we know who we belong to, which is Christ Jesus. Because that spirit of lust is coming back seven times as strong. The spirit of cussing is coming back seven times as strong. That spirit of being in debt is coming back seven times as strong. That spirit of drug use is coming back seven times as strong. So, you better make sure you know who you are because the enemy will be patient. If that spirit which you used to have gets a hold of you, the Bible says that you will be in worse shape this time. Anoint yourself today and everyday to make sure the old man in you doesn't come back!

"YOU'RE ALREADY BLESSED, LET THEM WASTE THEIR TIME HATING!"

Isn't God awesome? Let me ask again, isn't God awesome? Has He done anything for you today? If you think He hasn't, then do this: just stop breathing! Okay, now ... this is the day the LORD has made for us, let us be glad and rejoice and be blessed in it. In spite of what's going on this morning at your job or wherever you're reading this, you are blessed! You are blessed even as your enemies are trying to stop the process. Know this, once the LORD makes up His mind to bless you, it doesn't matter if they set traps for you, it doesn't matter if you are depressed, it doesn't matter if you are not feeling your best, it doesn't matter if you just got some bad news, just receive it. Don't allow people around you to make you feel as if you are not blessed or not going to be blessed. Just let them continue to hate on you as you praise the

LORD! Let them look in amazement. The enemy will sit at his board meeting and ask those who he sent to hate on you, "Didn't you attack their finances? Didn't you attack their family? Didn't you attack their job? Didn't you attack their friends to make them turn on them?" But if you can keep praise through these attacks and get ready for the LORD as He starts your new season, then you will be all right!

Scripture of the Day:

> Now it shall come to pass, if you diligently obey the voice of the LORD your God, to observe carefully all His commandments which I command you today, that the LORD your God will set you high above all nations of the earth. And all these blessings shall come upon you and overtake you, because you obey the voice of the LORD your God: Blessed shall you be in the city, and blessed shall you be in the country.
>
> Deuteronomy 28:1–3 (NKJV)

> The LORD will cause your enemies who rise against you to be defeated before your face; they shall come out against you one way and flee before you seven ways. The LORD will command the blessing on you in your storehouses and in all to which you set your hand, and He will bless you in the land which the LORD your God is giving you.
>
> Deuteronomy 28:7–8 (NKJV)

Listen, just receive it! God has already mapped it out for you. God has already put the blueprint of your blessing in place. It's already completed. And nothing can stop what the LORD has for you. Your enemies shall stand in the same room as the LORD blesses you and then they will scatter from you like roaches when the lights are turned on. Keep praising the LORD. Get a praise going knowing that you are already blessed, because you are! The haters are trying to distract your praise so you will stop believing that God has something for you, but they don't know how far you have come. You've come too far to stop now. The LORD has commanded that you are blessed. He didn't say that you will be blessed if you've been in church all your life. He didn't say that you will be blessed if you've never made a mistake. He didn't say you will be blessed if you've never felt like giving up or if you've felt defeated once before. He just wants you to obey His voice! Obey His commandments. People will try and hinder you by what you've done in the past, but the LORD does not remember your past. He's more concerned with your future. Get an "in spite of" praise! In spite of past failures; in spite of haters; in spite of what your bank account says; in spite of overdue bills; in spite of your job; in spite of your co-workers; in spite of your boss, in spite of people; in spite of where you live; in spite of what you drive; in spite of riding the city bus; in spite of…!

"YOU'RE FUTURE IS AHEAD OF YOU ... STOP LOOKING BACK!"

Tell yourself today, there is still hope! Just when you thought it was over, God showed up and showed off. I know you may feel you're not where you want to be in life. You may not have the job you want. You may not be making the money you want. You may not have the car you want. You may not live where you want to live. You may not even have the spouse you wanted but know that God has you right where He wants! If you can just hold on; if you can just stay focused on the LORD and not your situation, God will work it out. The Word says that the last will be first and the first will be last. So, if you feel as if you have always been in the rear; if you feel as if you have always been the last to get something, know that God is turning your situation around. With God you have hope. With God you have a future, regardless of what your track record says, regardless of what your past says, and regardless of what people say. With God there's still hope! Here's a sign to know that you still have hope: you're reading this writing! Many people will not see this day, but you have the opportunity to change your situation, because you're still alive!

Scripture of the Day:

> For I know the thoughts that I think toward you, says the LORD, thoughts of peace and not of evil, to give you a future and a hope. Then you will call upon Me and go and pray to Me, and I will listen to you. And you will seek Me and find Me, when you search for Me with all your heart.
>
> Jeremiah 29:11–13 (NKJV)

If we can change our focus, that will conquer half the battle. Because of the situations and circumstances we are in, we often say to ourselves that we have no future. If you can just take a quick look back and see where you have come from and understand that you are still going, then you will be able to realize that you have a future ahead of you. God already spoke thoughts of peace and not confusion, thoughts of peace and not of evil, thoughts of peace and not strife into our lives. He spoke it, now live it. He said pray and He will listen. He may not respond when you want, but He will not let you go under. Hold onto His word. Hold onto His hand and don't let go! Regardless of what life has shown you up to this point, know that God is right there with you and He wants to help you. But you must ask. He will not force Himself on you. Try Him. Everything else has failed. Everyone else has let you down. Now try the LORD! Know this, once you try Him and He blesses you, then that's not the time to go back to what you were doing. Now go and live! Not because I said so, but because you are still alive!

"ARE YOU SUFFERING FROM SOMETHING TODAY? IF SO, THEN YOU'RE IN THE RIGHT POSITION!"

When you read this today, before you think I'm crazy for what I'm about to tell you, just hear me out. If you are going through something right now, God may be trying to get the real 'you' out of that situation. For God to mold you into the person He really and truly wants you to be, He will allow some things to happen in your life to get that which is in you to be released. So, you should actually praise God for your troubles. You should praise God for your trials and tribulations. Understand that when you go through something, the more intense the circumstance, the more of a blessing God has for you. Your blessing is measured by your circumstance. That's why you go through things that seem like they are going to break you. If you can trust God and the key part of it is, if you can continue to praise God, then He will strengthen you, perfect you, and bless you all at the same time. The blessing is actually already there. It's up to your faith in God to make it a reality. Trust Him through your troubles, if you can stand to be blessed.

Scripture of the Day:

> But may the God of all grace, who called us to His eternal glory by Christ Jesus, after you have suffered a while, perfect, establish, strengthen, and settle you.
>
> 1 Peter 5:10 (NKJV)

God never said that you wouldn't suffer. God never said that times wouldn't get rough. God never said that you would have circumstances and issues that would cause pain and discomfort. But He did say that because you are called to His eternal glory, that He will settle you! We are called to His eternal glory, which means that we will be with God forever and His glory will overcome the suffering. Your pain and sorrow, it too shall come to pass. Your trials and tribulations, it too shall come to pass. Your suffering, it too shall come to pass. If you can trust the word of God and hold onto it and know that you will suffer momentarily, and know that going through God is already perfecting you, strengthening you, and settling you. Also know that if you can stand to be blessed by God, then you will go through some things. Keep trusting in the LORD! Stay in prayer! You determine your own outcome. The enemy can't do it. Your haters and enemies can't do it. It's up to you! God sees your hurt, but know that He is trying to get the real you out of you!

THOUGHT OF THE DAY
"JUST WHEN THEY THOUGHT THEY HAD YOU!"

In these times, we have to be very careful who we come in contact with. We have to be very careful who we share our ideas with. We have to be very careful who sits next to us in church, who we invite over for dinner, and who we laugh and joke with on a daily basis. For the haters are out and they are out to do one thing: to assassinate our character! Yes, they'll hate on you because you got that promotion. Yes, they'll hate on you because you got that new car. They'll even hate on you when you start to praise the LORD. But all that isn't what they really hate. They hate who you serve, and if they can take down your character then they'll feel as if you are exposed! But aren't you glad that the God we serve is a forgiving God? Aren't you glad that He washes away all the sins of our lives and they are never brought back to our attention? You know those folks who know about your past and every time there's a crowd, they want to bring it up? Look around you, they are there! When you were rolling with them, it wasn't a problem. But now that you've made changes and different choices in your life, all of a sudden it's a problem. Listen, just keep moving in God and watch your character, it's under attack!

Scripture of the Day:

> He sent from above, He took me; He drew me out of many waters. He delivered me from my strong enemy, From those who hated me, For they were too strong for me. They confronted me in the day of my calamity, But the LORD was my support. He also brought me out into a broad place; He delivered me because He delighted in me.
>
> Psalm 18:16–19 (NKJV)

Listen, I'll be brief. They can set traps. They can hate on you. They can lie and talk about you. They can spread all kinds of untrue gossip about you, but God has already delivered you from them. God is your support. Because God resides in you, He will not allow you to be consumed by those who mean you no good. Keep praising the LORD. Keep trusting in Him. Don't allow your enemies to distract your praise. Your praise is what will determine the blessing, for when the praises go up, the blessings come down! If you can't send anything up, don't expect much to come down. Stay focused on your season and what God has called you to do!

"JUST WHEN YOU WANTED TO THROW IN THE TOWEL, GOD HID IT!"

The spirit of giving up is in the air like never before. The enemy knows how close you are to your breakthrough. He knows how close you are to your new season. He cannot make you give up, but he can put all kinds of thoughts in your mind to make you give up. I know things may seem dim right now. I know things aren't going your way. You may be overcome with bills and debt. You may be ill. You may feel like your children are not going in the right direction in life and giving up seems to be so easy. That's just it! Because it's so easy to give up, you should go the other way. Your blessing will be measured by what you are going through. In other words, the more you endure, the more God is going to bless you! So trust in the LORD and call on those issues. Call on those problems. Call on those setbacks and understand that God will not allow you to give up, even when you want to!

Scripture of the Day:

> Commit your way to the LORD, Trust also in Him, And He shall bring it to pass. He shall bring forth your righteousness as the light, And your justice as the noonday. Rest in the LORD, and wait patiently for Him; Do not fret because of him who prospers in his way, Because of the man who brings wicked schemes to pass. Cease from anger, and forsake wrath; Do not fret–it only causes harm. For evildoers shall be cut off; But those who wait on the LORD, They shall inherit the earth.
>
> Psalm 37:5–9 (NKJV)

Aren't you glad the LORD will take the towel of submission that you have and hide it from you? Just when you wanted to throw in the towel, the LORD hid it from you and will allow you to taste just a small amount of what your prosperous season will be like if you stay in the game. Just wait on the LORD! Just keep a praise going in spite of your surroundings, regardless of what is trying to overtake you. Just wait on the LORD! He may not come when you want, but He's never late. Just when the thought of throwing in the towel seemed like the best option for you, God stepped in. If you don't believe me, then how are you still here?

THOUGHT OF THE DAY
"WHO HAS A POPEYE PRAISE?"

just had to share this with you all. God put this in my spirit as I was watching this cartoon. Do you remember Popeye? He was the muscle man who sought out help in times of trouble. Well, here's a twist. Check it out!

Olive Oyl = your prosperity/your new season

Popeye = you

Spinach = Holy Spirit

Bluto = the enemy

What you have to do is fill in the places where you see the cartoon character with the names above. Popeye likes what he sees in Olive Oyl. Popeye tries to get with Olive Oyl. Popeye can't wait until the day he gets with Olive

Oyl. Often, Olive Oyl gives Popeye a glimpse at what he will get when he reaches her, but Popeye has to keep believing that he will get with Olive Oyl. Now, here comes Bluto trying to distract Popeye from getting to Olive Oyl. Bluto really doesn't like Olive Oyl, he just doesn't want Popeye to get to her. Bluto sets all kinds of traps and sends all kind of people to try and hinder Popeye from getting with Olive Oyl. Bluto beats on Popeye, sends all kinds of demons after Popeye to wear him down and discourage him from trying to get to Olive Oyl. Popeye hangs in there and tries to hold on, and he keeps getting beat down and beat up. Popeye can't deal with Bluto. Popeye realizes that he can't do this on his own. Popeye then says, "That's all I can stanz, I can't stanz, no more!" Popeye then gets the spinach, eats it, gets it deep down in his belly, and the spinach empowers him. Popeye is now able to defeat Bluto with the assistance of the spinach.

Did you all follow me in this? The enemy is trying to distract you from what God has already promised you. Just hold on to what God has promised you and don't let go; God can't lie. It's coming, just hold out for it. Don't give up. Don't give in. You are too close! Get a Popeye praise going right now, wherever you are reading this, and let the enemy know you're not going to take anymore and you are going to call on your Father!

"WHAT OR WHO'S IN YOUR HOUSE TODAY?"

Today, let's recognize what is living in our homes. You see, you need to find out what's in your home, so then you'll be able to get rid of it. You can't get rid of what you don't know is there. The one spirit you should have in your home is the Spirit of the Living God. You should wake up thanking God for another day. You should go to your kitchen thanking God for food. You should take out your clothes, thanking God that you have clothes to put on your back. If you have children, you should thank God that your children are safe and sound on this day. You may be facing situations today and it doesn't seem like you will make it through, but just have the faith and trust that God will come through for you once again. If the wrong spirit gets into your home, then it affects you, your family, and those who come in contact with you. Prayer starts at home. If necessary, walk through your home praying out loud.

Scripture of the Day:

> Surely goodness and mercy shall follow me All the days of my life; And I will dwell in the house of the LORD Forever.
>
> Psalm 23:6 (NKJV)

If you look over your shoulder, you will see that you are being followed. If you trust in the LORD, He says that goodness and mercy shall follow you all the days of your life. Every time you're in that situation and you make it out, just look who's following you. Every time something is trying to consume you or someone is trying to keep you bound, just take a look around and see who's following you. You made it out of that car accident without a scratch because of who was following you. What should have killed you a long time ago and you still can't figure out how you made it out, it was because of who was following you. Now, with that we need to know that depression and God can't be in the same house. Self-pity and God can't be in the same house. Poverty and God can't be in the same house. Sickness and God can't be in the same house. In order to dwell in the house of the LORD forever, you first need to know what's in your house! And even if your house is clean right now, know that the attack is coming, but you have a weapon to keep it out! Do your spring cleaning in all the seasons. Keep prayer in your house at all times. Don't just pray when something isn't right. Rather, store up some prayers in the cabinets, so when something comes up and you're too weak to pray, the prayers that you stored up will be ready to get rid of what shouldn't be in your house! Don't give up!

THOUGHT OF THE DAY
"I'M GOING THROUGH ... ALL THE WAY THROUGH!"

There are many who are going through something on this very day. But if you read today's Thought of the Day again and read it one more time, you'll see the key word. The key word is "through." Your faith has already worked in your favor. If you notice, most of the time people say, "Well, I'm going through something right now." Notice that they don't say, "Well, I'm in something right now and I'm stuck." When you say that you are going through, you are actually saying that there are some rough bumps in the road, but you're coming out of it. One of the keys to your success is how you speak. If you can speak of your season, then that's where you'll end up. But if you complain and sit around and just sulk and feel pity on yourself by having a pity party, then that's what your outcome will be. Regardless of what people may have said about you, in spite of the lies, even if your bills are more than your paycheck from week to week, trust the LORD and speak victory into your future.

Scripture of the Day:

> Yea, though I walk through the valley of the shadow of death, I will fear no evil; For You are with me; Your rod and Your staff, they comfort me.
>
> Psalm 23:4 (NKJV)

God is saying that there will be rough times in your life and you will face difficulties, but if you allow Him to walk with you, He will comfort you. What we often do is try and figure out our situations and circumstances ourselves. Unfortunately, the LORD will just step back because what you are saying is that you can handle your problems yourself. But if you call on Him in times of trouble, He will show up and show off. Keep your trust in Him and if people call you crazy for calling on Him, if they isolate themselves from you because you want to seek a higher power, then let them go. Because the one thing you will find out about people is they will be right there with you when you have money, when times are going fine, when you are spending your money, with you in the clubs, even with you at church, but as soon as something happens and you're down and out, just watch how they will bail out on you. Stay focused on the LORD, for He will never leave you nor forsake you!

THOUGHT OF THE DAY
"NOW IS NOT THE TIME TO BE QUIET!"

On this day, let us try something different. Even if things aren't going right, let's focus on what *is* going right. You may be saying, "Well, there's nothing going right in my life at this moment." Well, I'm here to say that there is something going right for you. You have life this morning! I received an email from a friend of mine stating that they were playing basketball, just a pickup game with some friends. They were at church when this happened. One of the young men playing, who had just turned thirty years old, stopped and collapsed. He had a heart attack and died instantly. We often complain about things going on in our lives, but at least we have life. This could have been the day where someone was getting their eulogy message together for your family regarding you! But we have life today. Isn't that good enough to rejoice and be glad?

Scripture of the Day:

The dead do not praise the LORD, Nor any who go down into silence. But we will bless the LORD From this time forth and forevermore. Praise the LORD!

Psalm 115:17–18 (NKJV)

Listen, praise the LORD right now for keeping you safe thus far, for watching over you throughout the night when you slept, for keeping our children safe, and for blessing you with life today. Praise the LORD until you take your last breath, for we do not know when the death angel will come for us, but if we can get a praise going, our time could be extended. Remember King Hezekiah? The prophet Isaiah told him it was his time to die but because he focused on praising God, his life was extended an additional fifteen years. Today might have been the day for us to check out of here, but because we took time out to praise the LORD, in spite of what's going on in our lives, the LORD saw our praise and restored us. The LORD saw our praise and kept the death angel away on this day! Break out of that somber mood that the enemy wants to keep you in and just start to praise the LORD for His mighty works. Start praising Him for what He's about to do in your life. There's a new season coming to a theatre near you! Just receive it.

THOUGHT OF THE DAY
"KEEP THAT MIRROR CLEAN!"

I was telling someone to keep their mirror cleaned up and ready to be used at any given point in time. Here's what I mean. Often, we are so caught up in what's going on around us. We are so willing to help our neighbor, and there is nothing wrong with that, but when we get down, when things seem to be overcoming us, when we are going through, who is there to help us? I've learned to be like David. The Bible says that David encouraged himself (1 Samuel 30:6 NKJV). When there's no one there to lift you up, when your friends look at the caller ID and won't answer because they don't want to hear your problems, when you email someone and you know they read it but they don't respond and they have the out of office reply set up, you need to be able to encourage yourself! Be like David and encourage yourself when everyone else is too busy for you. This is when you pull out that mirror and dust it off and look in it and what you see is who needs to be encouraged today!

Stop calling on Ray-Ray to help you and stop emailing Susie to help you. Stop looking for June-Bug on the block to try and get you out of that financial situation. Start encouraging yourself through Christ who has strengthened us! If you have to preach a sermon to the mirror, then you do that and understand that once you can encourage yourself, you are a better tool for the LORD to use to encourage someone else.

THOUGHT OF THE DAY
"SHUT YO MOUTH MONTH!"

Follow me. God shared this with me. He said that I don't trust Him enough! There are some things going on right now that I was trying to figure out on my own and not allowing God to get into the mix, but through my own thick head, I realized that the battle is not mine. Listen, Christian folks go through stuff too! So then I said, "LORD, but what about those around me?" And here's where I got the "Shut yo mouth" from. This is "Shut yo mouth" month! I don't necessarily mean you, but the haters around you. God is about to do something so great in our lives in this month that the haters will have nothing else to do but shut their mouths. This is the scripture God spoke into me to share. Make sure you read part B of the Scripture!

Scripture of the Day:

> No weapon formed against you shall prosper, And every tongue which rises against you in judgment You shall condemn. This is the heritage of the servants of the LORD, And their righteousness is from Me," says the LORD.
>
> Isaiah 54:17 (NKJV)

You see, God is saying that the weapon will be formed. The haters will set the traps. They will lie on you. They will gossip about you, but it will not prosper. All they are really doing is keeping you in prayer because when they set the traps, you need to pray to get through. When they lie, you need to pray to get over it. When they gossip, you need to pray to press on. In the midst of them doing this to you, they are actually making your relationship with God that much closer. But it's part B of the scripture, don't miss it. Every time they rise up and speak against you, the LORD says He will shut them up! He will condemn them. He will take care of it. Keep praising Him. Let them call you crazy. You're crazy for the LORD. Let them say you think you're all that. You're all that to God! Just keep your praise and God will shut them up. This is "Shut yo mouth" month and God is the one shutting folks up! Praise Him and let me leave you with this word. The enemy has dished out all the tricks. You've seen all he can do, but the difference is he's now using new faces to do the same old tricks! Stay in prayer!

THOUGHT OF THE DAY
"COME OUT THE CLOSET!"

Isn't it funny, when a gay man or lesbian woman comes out of the closet how they are never ashamed to show who they are? It doesn't matter who's around. It doesn't matter where they are. They are not ashamed to show who they are. If you were to ask them if they were gay or not, they would boldly state that they are and confess that they are proud of it. Now, my point is this, isn't it also funny that some people who say they are Christians will not admit it unless they are in the four walls of the church? You know those folks who will seek you out in church and give you a hug and recite the church slogan, "I love you in Jesus' name!" Those words are equivalent to a slogan if they aren't sincere when being said. Those same folks will see you at the mall or the movies or at a restaurant and you can speak to them and they will look at you as if they never saw you before in their lives. You know these folks. They are ashamed to admit they are Christians outside of the church!

Scripture of the Day:

> For whoever is ashamed of Me and My words in this adulterous and sinful generation, of him the Son of Man also will be ashamed when He comes in the glory of His Father with the holy angels.
>
> Mark 8:38 (NKJV)

It's just that simple. If you are ashamed of Christ in this life and refuse to acknowledge Him, then when your time comes to face Him, He will also be ashamed of you. It's time for Christians to come out of the closet. All kinds of people are coming out of the closet with their particular lifestyles, except Christians! It's time for the people of God to come out and start to acknowledge Him for His works. Don't be ashamed to mention Him wherever you go. Don't be ashamed to admit that if it had not been for the Lord on your side you would have exited stage left a long time ago. Let us come out of the closet serving Him. And let us serve Him with gladness at all times, not just when we are in church or around the pastor or at the prayer service. But acknowledge Him at work, at your child's PTO meeting at school, in the grocery store, and even when you're out just hanging with friends. When your time comes to die and you face Him, He will already know if you were ashamed of Him or not. Let's be an example for the generation following us, so they will know what they need to do; seek the Lord at all times and do not be ashamed!

THOUGHT OF THE DAY
"YOU ARE THE WAY OF YOUR BREAKTHROUGH!"

Because we are safe today, because we are alive today, because we can still lift our hands in spite of what's going on in our lives, should let you know that you are that much closer to your breakthrough! God is not finished yet. Just when you thought He was finished with you, think again. Now that you have made it closer to your breakthrough means you must continue to praise Him. You must continue to worship Him. Don't stop now! You've come too far to give up now. Every time you feel like giving up, just take a moment and get away from yourself. You may feel like giving up. You may feel like it's time to throw in the towel. You may feel like your problems and issues are consuming you, but if you can get away from you and let your spirit start praising, then you will be that much closer to your miracle.

Scripture of the Day:

> You therefore must endure hardship as a good
> soldier of Jesus Christ.
>
> 2 Timothy 2:3 (NKJV)

It has been spoken that to be a good soldier of Christ, you must endure hardship. Christ is telling us that we will endure some things over our life span that will not be easy. Rough times are coming. Tough times are coming. Stormy days are ahead. But if you can hold on, if you can hold out, if you can keep praise, then you will make it through. Stop spending so much time praising your circumstances. Stop complaining about what's going on. The word already spoke that we will endure hardship, but it did not say that it would consume us. God has given the victory to us. God has placed us over hardship and God has given us the championship belt! Every time you praise Him, you get that much closer to your miracle. It's just that easy. Start praising God right now. Don't even look around to see who is looking. Just take about sixty seconds to praise Him for what He's doing and what He's about to do, for He's worthy to be praised!

THOUGHT OF THE DAY
"DO YOU REALLY LOVE HIM/HER?"

Let's assume it is St. Valentine's Day! This is the day you are supposed to show your loved one how much you truly love them. On this day, we usually share flowers with our loved ones. We usually go out to dinner. We usually have heart-shaped candy and treats for our loved ones, but I have a question: How much do you really love your mate? If you truly love your mate then they must be your best friend first, then your mate second. You must be able to share everything with them. You must feel comfortable around them. You must be able to communicate with them. But will you die for them? To make a relationship work, you must have godly love for that particular person. And godly love is when you will lay down your life for that person. So make sure you are with your soul mate. Make sure that you have committed your life to the one who will lay down their life for you. I am not advising individuals who are already married to divorce their spouse. If you have that person, then you can truly be able to say, "Happy Valentine's Day!" And if you are single today and seeking a mate, my advice to you is not to rush. Allow God to get that person for you that will treat you with respect and love you until the very end. If you rush it and choose someone, then you will only have a "temporary love." God wants you to have an "eternal love!" Trust in Him.

Scripture of the Day:

> Greater love has no one than this, than to lay down one's life for his friends.
>
> John 15:13 (NKJV)

Now after you've read this scripture, do you truly love your mate? Or does your mate truly love you? And the love I'm speaking on is godly love, not that love that lasts for three months and then it's gone. God already knows your heart and He knows your mate's heart. Even if you say you will do this, but are not sincere about it, you will only be fooling yourself and your mate. Once you've found that person who will lay down their life for you, being in love is a beautiful thing, but if you have anything less than that, then it's not godly love. The word says there is no greater love than one to lay down their life for his best friend. You may love that person, but what you need is that greater love God refers to. You don't have to wait until February 14th to show your mate how much you love them. Everyday should be February 14th. Have a special day today!

THOUGHT OF THE DAY
"I WILL TO DO GOOD, BUT EVIL LURKS!"

thank God for you all today! If no one else tells you this today, know that I love you! Have you all noticed that most of the times when you seek to do good, somehow evil lurks? Have you noticed that most of the times when you have it in your heart to do good, something happens and you end up being upset? Well that's because there's a test placed upon you. The Bible says that wherever good is, evil lurks. The test is, are you willing to proceed with doing good, regardless of how ticked off you got while trying to do good? You know how we are, we may have good in our hearts, but if what we were intending on doing something for someone and they somehow irked our nerves? Are you still willing to proceed with what you originally planned? Let me give you an example. You go to work today and you plan on giving your boss a sandwich from the breakfast wagon. Before you get the sandwich, your boss calls you in the office and tells you that you will not be getting that promotion. After hearing that, will you still be able to buy your boss that breakfast sandwich? That's the test! Can you overlook what was meant for evil and still do good?

Scripture of the Day:

> For the good that I will to do, I do not do; but the evil I will not to do, that I practice. Now if I do what I will not to do, it is no longer I who do it, but sin that dwells in me. I find then a law, that evil is present with me, the one who wills to do good.
>
> Romans 7:19–21 (NKJV)

Understand that it is not you, but the sin in you that does this whenever you seek to do good, but you end up committing a sin. This is why we must keep praise on us like an ID! Our praise must be like American Express–"Never leave home without it"–for this world is of sin. Don't think you're the only one who messes up. We all mess up and often we end up messing up when we intentionally meant to do good. You must press towards the mark. You must continue on with the good that is in your heart. Don't allow the evil that lurks to control your life. You can't give up on God. If the good you seek to do turns out not so good, then you must still continue to praise the LORD for what your heart sought out to do and not what you actually did. Keep praise in your mouth in spite of what may be going on around you. Trust the LORD!

THOUGHT OF THE DAY
"WHO ARE YOU TRYING TO PLEASE?"

Start this day off knowing that you need to please the LORD more so than you are trying to please people. First, let me stop and ask us all to give God praise for all He has done, all He's doing, and all He's going to do in our lives. Just when you thought it was all over, new life was put in you. You have been restored. Now, let us get back to pleasing God before man. Often we try to please our boss, we try to please our co-workers, we try to please our family, and we even try to please ourselves more than trying to please God. Our order of focus is all wrong if this is the case. God should be number one on the pleasing list for all He has done for us. That man couldn't do it. That woman couldn't do it. That job couldn't do it. When you were really down and out, it was only God who could do it. Matter of fact, it was only God who wanted to do it. This is why we need to continue to praise Him in spite of others. Don't allow others, by trying to please them, make you miss out on what God truly has for you. People will make you miss your blessing while you are trying to please them. Stay focused on God!

Scripture of the Day:

When a man's ways please the LORD, He makes
even his enemies to be at peace with him.
Proverbs 16:7 (NKJV)

Just please God and everything else will fall in line. Therefore, when working those long hours at work, praise God for it. Don't do it in order to move up the corporate ladder, because if you can trust God and continue to praise Him, you will be able to move up higher doing less! Okay, you missed it. When your boss calls you in the office and gives you additional work, know that you need to feed your subconscious that God is blessing you. Because just think, if there was no work, then your employer would need to lay off. Also know that, because you can please God with your praise and worship, your haters will even make peace with you. With your praise, don't be surprised if you receive an email from someone you know never liked you. With your praise, don't be surprised if someone you know means you no good blesses you with something. Don't be surprised if with your praise, your boss gives you a raise that the company can't even afford. Just keep praise in you. Don't allow the everyday circumstances and situations keep you quiet. Trust God and please Him and watch how everyone and everything around you will change. You must understand that you have it in you. What is that you ask? Praise! Please

God and whoever doesn't like it, then oh well. You've come too far to miss the mark.

"I DARE YOU TO SHARE THIS!"

I was in my car, I put a CD in, and it was the song I needed to hear. I'm sharing it with you because it was so strong in my spirit to share. I put the CD in and there it was: "I pray for you, you pray for me ... I love you, I need you to survive! I won't harm you, with words from my mouth ... I love you; I need you to survive!" Listen, the words are powerful. This song is on Hezekiah Walker's CD. Even though I don't know you all personally, it doesn't mean I don't need you to survive. I need you! Don't give up!

LORD, touch all those right now, even those with the hard hearts. Lose that spirit of rebellion and enter in LORD and let them know that Troy needs them to survive! All because we are part of your heavenly body, LORD! Just look around wherever you are right now. Look at the person in the next cubicle at your job. They may need to hear this.

They may have been at that point of giving up. Just tell them, "I need you to survive!"

Scripture of the Day:

Now you are the body of Christ, and members individually.

1 Corinthians 12:27 (NKJV)

When you have an injury to your legs, you need to walk. You may desire to walk, but your legs hurt so bad that you can't walk. You need your legs to assist you in what you desire to do, which is walking or running. The same thing occurs in the spirit. We need everyone, including that broken person; that person who wants to give up; that person who lost a job; who lost their momma/daddy; that person who lost a child; that person who is struggling with an addiction; that person who is one step closer to living on the street. We need these people because we are one in the same body. And just like we would pray for that injured leg to heal so we can walk again, we need to pray for that person. Even if it's just giving them a hug, let them know you love them and you need for them to survive.

"PRAISE HIM UNTIL IT HURTS!—AND BE REWARDED!"

Today we should have a praise like this was the day we stepped into our breakthrough! Who has that praise? Who's waiting for their season? Well, if you can get a praise going in spite of what your bank account says, in spite of the layoffs and unemployment, and in spite of yourself, then you will be blessed. Listen, don't allow people or even yourself to allow you to miss out on what God has for you. Often we feel as if God has forgotten about us because of our current situations, but God is allowing things to happen to you only to strengthen you and stretch your faith. Christ stretched out on the cross so we would be able to have our faith stretched out. Trust in the LORD and keep praise in your mouth.

Scripture of the Day:

Behold, bless the LORD, All you servants of the LORD, Who by night stand in the house of the LORD! Lift up your hands in the sanctuary, And bless the LORD. The LORD who made heaven and earth Bless you from Zion!

Psalm 134:1–3 (NKJV)

Don't stop praising the LORD! Even when you get news of the layoff, and when your bank sends back that returned check. Listen if you want God to repair these things, and you have to keep praise in you. Bless the LORD at all times; not just when you receive something from Him, but at all times. As hard as it may be at times, the quickest way to deliverance is through praise. Today, I would like for everyone to just take a moment and praise God for all He has done, all He is doing, and all He's going to do in our lives. There is more that He will give to us. We just have to walk in faith and not walk by what we see. Begin to walk in faith and get a praise going with your eyes shut. That way you won't care who's watching. You won't care what's going on around you. You won't care where you are because with your eyes shut, your focus will be truly on God. And when you open your eyes, just receive your new season. Be blessed today.

THOUGHT OF THE DAY
"START LIVING, WHILE YOU'RE ALIVE!"

I have a question for you. Who wants to spend the rest of their days in prosperity? Who wants the rest of their days to be filled with pleasure? I hope that everyone is saying that this is what they want for the rest of their lives and for their families. To obtain this, you must obey the LORD! It's just that simple. It's either you obey Him or you don't. There's no in between. You don't flip-flop when you feel like it. What I mean by flip-flop is, one day you love the LORD and want to obey His word and then the next day you want to do your own thing. When you do this, you are planting a negative seed, and if you continue, that negative seed will grow into something that will eventually destroy you. The saying is true, If you live by the sword, you die by the sword (Matthew 26:52 NKJV *paraphrased*)! If you feel like you don't need to obey the LORD and live your life the way you feel it needs to be lived, even if God spares you and you live a long time, that time will be spent in misery! Get on board, trust in God, and start living. There are many who are alive today, but are not living!

Scripture of the Day:

> If they obey and serve Him, They shall spend their days in prosperity, And their years in pleasures. But if they do not obey, They shall perish by the sword, And they shall die without knowledge.
>
> Job 36:11–12 (NKJV)

Listen. Never mind what yesterday brought to you. Never mind that person who keeps bringing up what you used to do. Never mind what your critics say about you. The time is now! God has spared your life up to this point, and if you can just look in the mirror, you will see a miracle. There is never a time when it's too late while you still have breath! Don't let anyone tell you it's too late. My own father gave his life to the LORD while on his death bed, and with the acceptance of Christ, the tears told us that his life was spared and He was heaven bound! Keep moving but make sure you're making the right moves. Move with God and obey His word. That doesn't mean you won't make a mistake. If you obey His word, then His word says, if you bring your sin to Him, He will cast it away forever. Trust Him. You've tried everything else. You've tried people. You've tried jobs. You've tried lotto. You've tried yourself. Now try God! Obey His word and start living while you're alive. Because once they close that coffin, it's over if you do not know Him and accept Him as your LORD and Savior!

"YOU'RE STILL HERE! EVEN AFTER ... "

don't want you to take what I'm going to share with you today the wrong way. Hear me out before you turn the page because you are discouraged. What I would like for you to do is to take a moment and just remember all those bad times that have occurred in your life over the years. Remember the rejections. Remember the bad credit. Remember the cheating spouse. Remember the abusive husband. Remember the bankruptcy. Remember the layoffs from work. Remember the haters. Remember the family members who don't like you. Remember the bounced checks. Remember the alcohol abuse. Remember the drug abuse. Remember the suicide attempts or thoughts. Remember when momma died. Remember when daddy died. Remember when any of your loved ones died. Remember those lonely nights. Remember being *that* close to living on the street.

Remember those rebellious children. Remember being hurt by loved ones. Remember growing up in that poor neighborhood. Remember growing up in that poor household. Remember not knowing where the next meal would come from. Remember all those things just for a moment. (I'm going somewhere with this.) After all that you've suffered, all that you've been through, after all that consumed you at one point or another in your life, you are still here!

Scripture of the Day:

And we know that all things work together for good to those who love God, to those who are the called according to His purpose.

Romans 8:28 (NKJV)

Just when the enemy thought he had you. Just when he thought you were going to give up. Just when the night came and with the night came tears, but the Bible says weeping may endure for a night but joy comes in the morning. How many of us thought we wouldn't see that next morning? God is proving Himself to us each day of our lives. We have come so far and been through so much, but even after all that, we are still here! Thank God for your troubles. The word says that it's good that I've been afflicted. Here's a good point: blessings happen in order. Before you wake up, you must first go to sleep. When you are awake, you get sleepy and weary which makes you want to go to sleep. The same thing occurs with blessings. You must first be broken; you must first go through some stuff and endure some things then you will be blessed. You can't get blessed first then go through. You will lose the blessing in the mess you're in. So today, remember to remember.

THOUGHT OF THE DAY
"IT'S YOUR TIME TO SEEK HIM!"

For this is the day! God made this day for you and me to rejoice and be glad in it. We could have been on the outside looking in, but God spoke to our organs and body functions and all the mechanisms that make our body work. Everything happened in order. Everything happened just at the right time. Everything took place for us to be able to not only open our eyes this morning, but for us to have use of our limbs, have eyesight, and be able to hear. We need to take advantage of this and not take it for granted. There's someone today who would love to trade places with you. Regardless of what you're going through right now, they would love to take on your issues. They would love to take on your situations and problems. They would love to be in debt. They would love to have people hating on them. They would love to have to ride the bus because they don't have a car. They would love to go to that job that seems to have no growth. If you don't think so, if you could, I would ask you to ride by your local hospital and ask those hooked to respirators and machines that keep them breathing if they would trade places with you! Or, ride by the cemetery and ask who wants another chance. Turn your complaints into praise!

Scripture of the Day:

He shall receive blessings from the LORD, And righteousness from the God of his salvation. This is Jacob, the generation of those who seek Him, Who seek Your face.

Psalm 24:5–6 (NKJV)

With all that's going on in the world, with drugs and violence on the rise, with the job market not where it used to be and unemployment on the rise, this is the time not to pout and give up. This is the time to seek Him! This generation of people needs to grab hold of Christ and understand that there is no life without Him. Yeah, you may be alive. Yeah, you may have material things. Yeah, you may have riches, but all that is temporary without Christ! All those things are being stored up for the generation that seeks Him. You can't get jealous when you see folks getting things and you're not. You can't get envious when you see people getting promotions at the job and you're not, especially when the people getting these things are not believers in Christ and are the most hateful people you know. Everything they are getting, they are getting for you! Keep a praise in your mouth and stay focused on Christ because you are part of this generation. Therefore, you need to seek Him, and He will place you above all that goes on in the world. Give Him praise right now, not because I said so, but because you can!

THOUGHT OF THE DAY
"JUST TO BE CLOSE TO YOU IS MY DESIRE!"

Here's a message from God! God brought this to my attention to share with you. Someone needs to hear this. Here's what I want you to do. In your quiet time, I want you to allow this song to minister to your spirit. This song is on the gospel recording artist Fred Hammond's CD. Come on "Just to be close to you / Just to be close to you / Just to be close to you / is my desire!" Sing that unto Lord! Now sing it again. Now sing it again. There's a breakthrough in this song. Come on... "Just to be close to you / Just to be close to you / Just to be close to you / is my desire." How many want to be close to the Lord this morning? Sing, people of God. Feed your spirit with this. Now, after you've ministered to your spirit, here's the part that blew my mind. Here's the part that brought out a shout in me. Here's the part that put the icing on the cake. After I sang that song a few times and as I began to worship the LORD, He then responded. If you minister that song correctly, He will come into your presence. The LORD responded by saying, "Just to be close to you / Just to be close to you / Just to be close to you / is My desire!" You see, God loves us so much that He will turn around and desire to be just as close to us as we want to be to Him! He loves you. Someone on this list needs to hear this today. He loves you! In spite of the money issues, in spite of the job issues, in spite of folks lying on you, in spite of folks trying to set you up, in spite of relationship problems and divorce, He loves you!

Quote of the Day:

"Just to be close to you … Just to be close to you … Just to be close to you … Is my desire!"

There's no scripture today. I'm just sharing what the LORD gives me. I believe in my heart that someone was about to give up and God spoke to me to share this to let that person know that God wants to be close to you just as you want to be close to Him! Someone needed to hear that God is still in control and that He loves them! I'm praying for you right now. I'm lifting you up right now. Listen. Stop looking at what you can see! You walk by faith and not by sight! Start walking with a blindfold, which symbolizes that you believe in the LORD and that you want to walk in the steps God has ordered for you. Just to be close to you is what God desires, but He can't get close if you focus on your issues and don't worship Him. Get ready for the transfer. Get ready to have your territory enlarged. It's tough right now only because God is about to do something so big in your life, and the enemy knows this, so he's trying to distract you and make you give up on God! But what the LORD promised ... somebody praise Him!

"TO RECEIVE SOMETHING NEW, YOU HAVE TO GIVE HIM SOMETHING NEW!"

It's time to move ahead! It's time to allow God to bless us mightily. For the Word says that He not only comes to give us life, but to give us more life. He comes to give us more than we can ever handle. He came not only so that our blessings will run over the cup, but who wants their saucers to run over? Those are the blessings from God that will run over the top of the cup onto the saucer, and the saucer can't even hold what God has for you!

You may notice in the second sentence I said *allow* God to bless us. You see, God is trying to bless us, but we stop what He is trying to do. That's right! It is not the enemy, not your haters, not your job, not your lack of money, not because you have bills. We are the reason why we miss out on what God has for us. Be glad that God is a God of second chances. But He is a God of third, fourth, fifth, sixth, and seventh chances. In other words, God will be back to bless you if you miss, and He'll come again and again and again if He has to wait until you get it right.

One of the most important things that keeps us from getting blessed, that keeps us from being taken to the next level by the LORD is that we have the same ole' praise! You may have praised Him to get where you are, but to go even higher you must get a higher praise! Don't worry about who is around. Don't worry about who is looking. Just get a new praise for the new day. Get a new praise for your new home. Get a new praise for your new money. And get a new praise for your new mercies… praise Him!

Scripture of the Day:

> Through the LORD's mercies we are not consumed, Because His compassions fail not. They are new every morning; Great is Your faithfulness.
>
> Lamentations 3:22–23 (NKJV)

Each day God breathes life into your lungs. He also places new mercies in your purse or wallet for the day. He knows that each day you will face something new. The enemy will come for you in a new way. He's tried to get to you over and over, but has failed (you're still here, so that lets me know he's failed). Since he failed on Thursday, he'll come again Friday. But the LORD has given you something new to fight him off! He has given you new mercies today. You need to get a new praise for what's going to happen today.

There might have been a fatal car accident awaiting you, cancer may have been knocking at your door, bankruptcy was awaiting you, but the LORD gave you new mercies to fight it off and all the LORD requires from you is praise. And when you praise Him, make sure it's not the same ole' praise from last week because last week's mercies may not be able to get you out of the trouble that face you today!

Listen, the word says that if you submit yourself to the LORD, the enemy will flee from you, but it doesn't mean that he won't come back. This is why God gives us new mercies each day; because He knows the enemy will be back for us. This is why we are given new mercies each and every day regardless of our situation. Regardless of what you are facing today, you have new mercies. It doesn't matter if you don't have money or if you live in a studio apartment. It doesn't matter. All that matters is the LORD has given you something new today, so He deserves something new!

THOUGHT OF THE DAY
"LET YOUR HEART NOT BE TROUBLED! PRAISE HIM FOR YOUR MANSION!"

For this is the day that the LORD has made for you! It doesn't matter what's going on in your life today. This is the day the LORD has made for you! Your bills may be overdue. Your bank account may be dwindling. Your job may be laying off employees. Yes, the economy is not in good shape, but in spite of all that, this is still the day the LORD has made for you! My point is if God says He's going to do something for you, it doesn't matter what the world thinks or what's going on in the world. You will receive it. Since today is the day He's made for you, just get ready to receive His blessings and keep your focus on God instead of what's going on around you! If He said it, it will happen. If He promised you, it will come to pass. Here's what you need to be doing in the meantime. You need to be praising

Him. You need to be worshiping Him in spirit and in truth. You need to be praying and fasting. Show the LORD that you trust in Him and not man. Don't allow your situation to throw you off track from praising Him. Stay focused today, for this is your day! Not because I said it, but because the LORD declared it!

Scripture of the Day:

> Let not your heart be troubled; you believe in God, believe also in Me. In My Father's house are many mansions; if it were not so, I would have told you. I go to prepare a place for you. And if I go and prepare a place for you, I will come again and receive you to Myself; that where I am, there you may be also. And where I go you know, and the way you know.
>
> John 14:1–4 (NKJV)

God does not want His people worrying and being stressed over things. He wants His people to know that He is coming back for them. If you believe in Christ, your heart should not be troubled. If you can trust in the LORD, your heart should not be troubled because with your belief comes healing. With belief comes prosperity. With belief comes joy. With belief comes deliverance. With belief comes peace. You just need to put in your mind and in your heart that you believe! Times will get tough. Situations will come in your life that will cause distractions that will try to hinder you, but let your heart not be troubled! God has already pre-pared blessings for you, and it's only you who can stop the mansion from being built. It's only you who can stop the blessings. Nothing, no one, no situation, no circumstance can stop what God has for you! If He said He will, then He will. Today, let's focus on God and not the troubling circumstances in our lives!

THOUGHT OF THE DAY
"TOO LATE DEVIL, GOD CHOSE ME FIRST!"

I asked the Lord, as I do everyday, to give me a word to share for the people of God and being chosen was what He shared with me again! Here's what He placed on my heart to share today. You see when you have defeated something you must first acknowledge it. You must first admit to yourself that it's there! You can deny something and then try to overcome it. Because the battle is not yours, you are more than a conqueror. You have overcome the enemy, but you must first acknowledge him.

Today I want you to write him a letter of victory! What do I mean? Well, here's my letter: Dear devil, I want to thank you for thinking so much of me. Thank you for messing with my finances. Thank you for messing with my relationship with my family. Thank you for my enemies who work for you. Enemy, I truly know that I'm a child of God. No weapon you form will prosper and the God I serve will take what you have formed and turn around and bless me. Thank you! Also, thank you for trying to trick me into serving you and not Christ because you only made our relationship that much closer. Everything you tried to do only prospered me that much more. Thank you for hating me! I'm covered by the blood of Christ and nothing can change that. Today I just wanted to acknowledge you and let you know that you have been defeated not because of me, but because of whom I serve. The battle is not mine. Take your issues up with my Daddy in Heaven! I end by saying, you're too late. I'm already chosen by Christ!

Scripture of the Day:

'You are My witnesses,' says the LORD,' And My servant whom I have chosen, That you may know and believe Me, And understand that I am He. Before Me there was no God formed, Nor shall there be after Me.'

Isaiah 43:10 (NKJV)

Listen, the LORD doesn't choose failures. The LORD doesn't choose those who are depressed. He doesn't choose those who are broke. My point is, because you have been chosen, you are victorious over all that try and hinder you. Here's the issue. Many of us focus on our past rather than where God is bringing us. That's where your faith has to kick in! That's when you have to adjust your glasses. I told someone the other day to use a divine glass cleaner on their glasses because they were focusing on what they saw instead of believing what God promised them! Know this: if He promised it to you, then it will happen. It took Joseph a long time to get his stuff back, but after a while, everything God had promised him came to pass. Sometimes you have to wait. It doesn't mean it's not going to happen, but you just have to wait for a minute. Trust the LORD and don't forget your letter to the enemy today. Acknowledge him and acknowledge that you are a child of God!

THOUGHT OF THE DAY
"WATCH YOUR STEP!"

For this is truly the day! Today we are going to watch where we are stepping. Today we are going to make sure we are on the righteous path that God has ordered for us. One of the reasons we are dealing with so much turmoil in our lives today is because we have gotten off track. The LORD speaks to us not to do something, but we take it in our own hands to do that very thing and then when we fail. When we get caught up in sin, we then ask the LORD for forgiveness. We wouldn't have to do that if we had only listened to Him in the first place. God has our steps ordered and He knows that from time to time we will get off track. That's why He gives us grace and mercy! But we must also understand that if we continue to step out of line, if we continue to take a left when God planned for us to go right, if we continue to do things in spite of God telling us not to, the grace that has been given to us can run out! How? God's grace will run out if we keep doing something over and over

OUT OF DEATH COMES LIFE

again after God told us to stop. Watch your steps today. Make sure you're walking in the steps God has ordered for you and you shall prosper! Be blessed.

> Moreover the law entered that the offence might abound. But where sin abounded, grace abounded much more, so that as sin reigned in death, even so grace might reign through righteousness to eternal life through Jesus Christ our LORD. What shall we say then? Shall we continue in sin that grace may abound? Certainly not! How shall we who died to sin live any longer in it?
>
> Romans 5:20–6:2 (NKJV)

Scripture of the Day:

> The steps of a good man are ordered by the LORD, And He delights in his way.
>
> Psalm 37:23 (NKJV)

Here's where we mess up. We walk, but we want to walk on our own. We do things and then ask for forgiveness. Have you ever done something, but before you did that very thing, you knew deep down inside that you shouldn't be doing it? You may feel all tingly inside because you know it's wrong, but you do it because it feels right for the moment and you don't really think of the consequences? This is when you have jumped off track. You have stepped out of line. The steps of the LORD did not have you going that way.

What you must also understand is that the steps He has for you will not be easy. This must occur in order for you to be taken to the next level. You should never get comfortable. You should never become dormant. You should always want more from the LORD! And as long as you can stay in line, you will be blessed and you will make the LORD glad! Continue to be praying for me as I do the same for you!

"IT'S TIME TO FILL UP ON HIS POWER!"

Today, I want to share with you that it's okay to admit that you are at a weak state in your life. It's okay to admit that your situations and circumstances have weakened you over the past months. It's okay because the way to be delivered and restored by the Lord is to first admit that you need Him. You see, God will sit on His throne and allow you to continue to go through things if He sees that you believe you don't need Him. He's such a gentleman that He won't intrude in your business if you don't want Him to. At some point, we all need the Lord. Don't allow the enemy to mess with your mind and tell you that you can do it on your own. The devil is a liar! Know that God only allows situations to happen to you to build your Faith in Him and to make your stronger in the word. When you to gain physical strength, you must first lift something heavy. You lift weights to gain muscle. In the spiritual realm, you must lift that which you are going through to gain spiritual strength. And no matter how heavy it gets, the Bible says that yet in all things you are more than a conqueror! Somebody praise Him today.

Scripture of the Day:

> He gives power to the weak, And to those who have no might He increases strength. Even the youths shall faint and be weary, And the young men shall utterly fall, But those who wait on the LORD Shall renew their strength; They shall mount up with wings like eagles, They shall run and not be weary, They shall walk and not faint.
>
> Isaiah 40:29–31 (NKJV)

Listen. Today, before you get to work or wherever it is you have to go, you need to stop at your local spiritual service station and get a refuel. The word today says, "He gives power to the weak and to those who have no might He increases strength." God will refuel you with His power. He will renew your energy level. He's like Gatorade. He'll restore all that your body has lost. The enemy thought he had you, but he should have taken you out long ago! This is the day that the LORD has made and you need to be glad and rejoice because God is about to restore your strength. And all you have to do is wait on Him. He may not show up when you want Him to, but He's never late! He's never lost a battle and He's never lost a fight. He's undefeated and He reigns over everything. Praise Him right now, and in the midst of your praise, He's going to restore your strength.

Even the young folks are going to get weary; even the young folks are going to faint at some point, but because you waited on the LORD, you'll be like the energizer bunny and keep going and going and going and going and going and going … Praise Him!

"TODAY'S BLUES VS. TODAY'S BLESSINGS!"

For this is the day! Keep telling yourself that. Keep acknowledging that each day the LORD brings you forth with life will be the day for your breakthrough. Listen. This is the start of something from God! Today is the first day of something. I don't know what, but it's from the LORD. Therefore, it's a blessing.

You are in the beginning of your season. You've made it through. This is not the day to give up. This is not the day to give in. This is not the day to lose hope. Somebody reading this is that much closer to their breakthrough. Somebody who has been asking the LORD for something is going to receive it on this day! Today represents your new season. You must not grow weary. You have to continue your praise. I know you're tired of some things. I know some folks have gotten on your last nerve. I know the job is stressing you. I

OUT OF DEATH COMES LIFE

know money just isn't right. But today, I say the new season begins. If God can bring you to it, He'll bring you through it. Don't allow the distractions to make you miss out now. You are too close! Start praising right now. The word says this is the day the LORD has made for you. Well let me paraphrase it a bit, this is the day that the LORD has made for you. Rejoice and be glad because you're in it. You could be on the outside of today looking in, but because of the twins, grace and mercy, and because of the fact that God is not going to allow you to succumb before blessing should let you know that this day is for you! Somebody who believes this is their day should give Him praise!

Scripture of the Day:

> And let us not grow weary while doing good, for in due season we shall reap if we do not lose heart.
>
> Galatians 6:9 (NKJV)

I know you may know this scripture and even if you don't, apply it to your day! Allow it to minister to what you are going through right now. What you're doing is not being done in vain. It's not going unnoticed. If you continue to labor for the LORD, you shall reap in due season. The reason why you haven't seen what God has for you is because it's not your time yet. But know that your time is coming and the most important thing is what to do while waiting. You must continue to wait with praise. You must continue to wait with faith. You must worship while waiting.

God is moving on your behalf. If not, what you are going

through right now would have, and probably should have, destroyed you. But God allowed you to see the pain you are dealing with right now only to bring you that much closer to your season. You must have pain first, before you can get blessed. For those who are dealing with something, for those who have issues, for those who are enduring pain and suffering right now, know that it's now time for your season. The enemy knows this, so he's trying to throw you off track. He's trying to make you believe that your season is not this close, but the devil is a liar! This is your day! Somebody start a praise! For this is a new day and it symbolizes that this is the beginning of something from God for you!

THOUGHT OF THE DAY

"I'M A BIT NERVOUS, BUT I STILL GOT PRAISE!"

I know there are times when you just feel outnumbered. You just feel like everyone and everything is against you! But you must have faith and trust in the LORD that you will overcome all that is against you. The word does say that if God be for you, then who can be against you (Romans 8:31 NKJV). Well, just start to live that way. Keep a song in your heart and praise in your mouth. As soon as you start to feel boxed in, as soon as you feel pressured, as soon as you start to feel like people are closing in on you, as soon as you start to feel as if your current situation is too much for you, here's what I want you to do: I want you to get a "Claustrophobic Praise!" Let me explain. Claustrophobic means the fear of being closed in. Well, this is to let you know that you can fear it, but still praise the LORD.

In spite of what's closing in on you, in spite of who's

trying to set traps for you, in spite of your overdue bills and the shut-off notices, or the situations that have come up and you just don't know how it's going to get done, you may have fear. You may fear that things are closing in, so get that "Claustrophobic Praise" going and trust the LORD that He will bring you out. He's only allowing this to happen to strengthen and test your faith in Him. He will not allow you to endure more than you can bear. Before you stop reading this, praise Him, and then keep reading. The time is now!

Scripture of the Day:

> The LORD is my light and my salvation; Whom shall I fear? The LORD is the strength of my life; Of whom shall I be afraid? When the wicked came against me To eat up my flesh, My enemies and foes, They stumbled and fell. Though an army may encamp against me, My heart shall not fear; Though war may rise against me, In this I will be confident.
>
> Psalm 27:1–3 (NKJV)

Let me just keep it real … you can be in the LORD all day and night, but there may be a time when you may experience fear, even if it's just for a moment. The word says you should not fear, but understand that our spirit may not fear, but the flesh may. Here's an example: You come from your annual physical and you just found out that you have terminal cancer. Your first reaction may be fear, but then you calm down and trust in the LORD to heal you. My point to this is, when you begin to fear, even if for a moment, overcome it with praise. You can praise Him even though you may have some fear, but you are still able to praise your way out. Your local bank sent you that letter about your accounts being negative and you have bills due, but still praise Him! You may not feel like going to work because yesterday was the day from hell, but still praise Him! People have been setting all kinds of traps for you because the enemy knows greatness is coming for you, but still praise Him!

Listen, you can praise the LORD to a point where He will not only restore you, but send the blessing on a quicker rate than it was originally suppose to get here. I'm going to keep praising Him regardless of what I can see because your faith will be your guide. Your Praise will be your guide and it will guide you to your promise! Keep praising Him in spite of the fear!

THOUGHT OF THE DAY
"MATURITY DOESN'T ALWAYS COME WITH AGE!"

Today the LORD told me to share with you there are people who grow old, but they don't grow up! We must understand that maturity does not come with age. That is why you have people around you who, according to their birth certificate, are considered an adult, but the way they act you would think they are in kindergarten or grammar school. I know you all know some folks like this. They may even be in the place where you work. **WARNING** Stay away from individuals who may act like this. Just keep them in prayer but try not to interact with them too much. Most of the time all they want is attention. What you must understand is that people who act in this manner are only trying to irk your nerves and keep you from receiving your promise from God! Don't fall into the traps they set. Don't play the games they want you to play and most of all, don't allow them to get on your nerves to the point where you get into a verbal confrontation with them. Just keep praying for them.

Scripture of the Day:

> When I was a child, I spoke as a child, I understood as a child, I thought as a child; but when I became a man, I put away childish things.
> 1 Corinthians 13:11 (NKJV)

Be aware that folks are still out there who have not put away their childish ways. These individuals can easily lure you into their drama by their actions. Keep your sensors up for these individuals and let your actions reveal your character. Therefore, do not get involved in what they may be trying to trap you in. Remember, it does not matter how old they are. It does not matter how long they have been on the job. It does not matter how long they have been a member at the church. In some cases, it does not matter how long you've been married to this person. If they have not put away those childish ways then they are only a roadblock to what God truly has for you. Just keep praying for those who act in this manner and keep trusting in the LORD and the direction He has for you!

THOUGHT OF THE DAY
"WHO HAS A LAY-A-WAY PRAISE?"

Who has a "Lay-A-Way" Praise? Here's what I mean: you know how you go to the store and you don't have enough money to purchase what you want, you put it on lay-a-way? What happens is, you pick out what you want and you can't afford it right at that very moment, so you bring the item to the lay-a-way section of the store and you give them the item and they put your name on it. They then tell you that you have a certain amount of time to pay it off, but no one else will get your item because according to the store, it's yours! The store has put faith in you that you will pay this off. The same thing occurs in the spiritual realm! If you can get a "Lay-A-Way" praise going, you're telling the LORD, I may not be able to afford it now, but You have enough faith in me that I will obtain it in given time. And the LORD will take your blessing and put it up for you, making sure your name is on it, and that no one else will be able to receive it. Come on. Get that praise going right now. The LORD has some stuff stored up for you.

Scripture of the Day:

> Ask, and it will be given to you; seek, and you will find; knock, and it will be opened to you. For everyone who asks receives, and he who seeks finds, and to him who knocks it will be opened.
>
> Matthew 7:7–8 (NKJV)

God wants you to try Him! He said that all you have to do is ask; all you have to do is seek and you shall find and knock on the door of opportunity and you shall receive! It has to be in His name's sake. The enemy wants you to believe that God has nothing for you; that the rut you may be in right now will last forever. But if you can get a "Lay-A-Way" praise going right now, in spite of what's going on in your life, understanding that you may not be able to handle your blessing right now or be ready for it, but because you asked, the LORD shall put your name on it until the time is right. No one else shall receive what's yours! Start the praise right now. Don't wait until you get to church on Sunday. Don't wait until you are at your last straw. Start it right now and store it up. For when the praises go up, you're that much closer to paying off your "Lay-A-Way" and the blessings will eventually come down. Just ask!

"TOO LATE SICKNESS, WE ARE HEALED!"

Let's pray for total healing today! Let us intercede for those who may have an illness or pains/sickness in their body. I was praying in church one day, and the Holy Spirit came upon me to let me know that there are people suffering all around you. You see, I care about people and their wellbeing. If someone hurts, then I hurt, and I felt the pain of people that particular day I was in church. God showed me how people are hurting; how people are sick, but here's the difficult part I saw. A lot of people are suffering or have a sickness but don't have anyone praying for them. Also, those people feel like no one cares, and because they continue to have their sickness, they are loosing faith in God healing them. Many are about to give up. Let's pray today. Pray for a supernatural healing to take place in whatever part of the country or world that you are in. Once you read this and you know of someone who is not feeling their best, even if the person just has a cold or flu, intercede in prayer for them because there's also healing for their soul!

Scripture of the Day:

> But He was wounded for our transgressions, He was bruised for our iniquities; The chastisement of our peace was upon Him, And by His stripes we are healed.
>
> Isaiah 53:5 (NKJV)

Do this: read that again! Now read it again … I'm going somewhere with this. When you read it, you have to know that God has already healed you or the person whom you have prayed for. Even though they still might have some symptoms, God is working in them or you because you simply asked for healing. If you see where it says, " … and by His stripes we are healed," the word "are" means it's already done! The tense of that word means it's a done deal, so the healing has already taken place. Just receive it for yourself and receive it for the individual or individuals who you prayed for. There's a healing right in this writing you're reading. Don't think that God can not work through these writings, because believing and having faith is the main ingredient to obtaining what you need from God!

When people tell you that others have passed away and have the same illness you have, when they tell you that this person didn't recover from what you may have right now, when the discouragement rises, just tell them, "By His stripes I am healed!" Speak it and mean it! You notice it doesn't say,

"…by His stripes you might be healed." No, God is trying to see how much faith we have in Him. Believe it, speak it, work it, use it, and yell it. Do whatever it is you have to do, but know it's a done deal! You're not going anywhere until God says so!

THOUGHT OF THE DAY
"LIVE TODAY! AND LET GOD HANDLE TOMORROW."

At the time of birth, we had no idea that our clock started ticking. We had no idea that when they make up our birth certificate and it's signed that our death certificate was also made up, but not signed. We want God to hold the pen to our death certificate. We want only His signature on it because if it's signed by the enemy, then that's where you will spend your eternity. We must live our lives to the fullest because we never know when our last breath will be taken. We could read the last page of these writings today. We could kiss our loved ones for the last time today. We could go to work for the last time today. Knowing this should make us have praise just in case it's time for us to leave here. Those who have chosen Christ as the head of their lives understand that they will eventually die, but those who have chosen Christ also believe that once this occurs, we will then be risen again to live with Him. We must enjoy life today and not put it off until tomorrow, because tomorrow may not come. Keep the praise!

Scripture of the Day:

> For the living know that they will die; But the dead know nothing, And they have no more reward, For the memory of them is forgotten.
>
> Ecclesiastes 9:5 (NKJV)

There are people walking around here that look alive and smell alive, but are just as dead as those who are already in the cemetery. Here's my point: I'm sure you all know some folks who complain about everything. All they do is stay mean and look mean all the time. They never have anything good to say. Even when you or someone else helps them, they are never appreciative. This is a person who is alive but dead in the spirit! Since they do not know Christ, it's as if they are just taking up breathing space. These are individuals we need to pray for. We cannot take their negativity personally. They just may not know any better. We have to at least pray that one day, before it's too late, they will see the light and choose to live while they are living. Oftentimes it's too late before an individual finds out how much life truly means. Let's live today! Let us not worry, but trust in the LORD. He has already done what needs to be done. Now is the time to praise Him until you can see His work. Don't stop now.

THOUGHT OF THE DAY
"TIME MACHINE PRAISE ... START IT NOW!"

Where you are right now–even if you have riches, even if you have everything you want, even if everything is going all right–God still wants to bring you even higher. Today, I want us to get a "Time Machine" praise! But what you must do is make sure you set the praise for the future. Oftentimes we get down and depressed, and it's because of our past. God has forgiven us so we now need to forgive ourselves and just start to praise the LORD for what He has for us in the future. When you enter this praise, you will be brought to the future and God will reveal to you what He has for you. This will be the incentive for you not to give up now. What you may be going through right now is a setup from God. Get that praise going ... just start thanking the LORD for what He's about to do in your life.

With this "Time Machine" praise, houses will be paid

off, debt will be paid off, healing will take place, relationships and marriages will be restored, and God will send you that husband/wife you wanted. With this praise, jobs will call you and promotions will be given to you, in spite of the job market. With this praise, all your enemies will assist you in going higher in Christ. Just when you thought you couldn't go any higher in Christ, God used your enemies to assist you in going higher. That's why the word says that your enemies will be your footstools...so just keep the praise! Stay focused on Christ. Don't allow the enemy to stop you. Because the enemy has peaked in your future and saw what God has for you, and he feels now is the time to go all out and try to have you stop you!

Scripture of the Day:

> I will praise You forever, Because You have done
> it; And in the presence of Your saints I will wait
> on Your name, for it is good.
>
> Psalm 52:9 (NKJV)

Start it right now. God is about to do something so miraculous in your life. I don't know who I'm speaking to, but I feel it. I'm receiving this word. Just when your haters thought they had you, just when the frustrations of your job were about to consume you, just when you thought your finances were so messed up that you wouldn't be able to pay for your next meal...here is God! Now with this miracle, you will need to get that "Time Machine" praise going. Praise Him for what He's about to do.

He's a very present help in the time of trouble. What this

OUT OF DEATH COMES LIFE

means is God will be right there for you before you get in that mess and still bless you while you're in that mess. With praise comes deliverance; with praise comes healing; with praise comes blessings … bless the LORD at all times, for His praises shall continually be in my mouth. Wait on Him with praise and receive what He has for you. The LORD has placed this word on me to share because He's done something for someone and you don't see it yet, but with that praise, it will come to pass. No matter what you're going through, just remember that God is only using you!

THOUGHT OF THE DAY
"IF YOU CAN BREATHE TODAY, PRAISE HIM!"

know there are many of you who are dealing with issues on this day. I know that many may have problems on this day. All kinds of things may be going on in your life today. You may have financial struggles, you may have issues at work, there may be people that are out to get you, you may have addictions, you may be having health issues ... whatever the case may be, there's something that is bothering you on this day. You may not even like your job, but you go there day after day to pay the bills. You may be having problems in your relationship, either with your spouse or children. Your bills may be more than your paycheck. You may feel like giving up is an option because you've been trying for so long to get ahead, but you seem to be going backwards. These things and many more seem to be hindering you today. Now, after all that, I'm here to tell you that you still should have praise!

You're probably saying, "Troy doesn't know what's going on in my life, so how can he tell me to praise the Lord?" Well, I'm really not the one telling you to praise the Lord ... the word of God is telling you that you should be praising the Lord! Don't believe me. See below.

Scripture of the Day:

Let everything that has breath praise the Lord. Praise the Lord!

Psalm 150:6 (NKJV)

This may sound like a silly request, but hear me out. If you can, take a deep breath ... only do this if you can. If you can, just inhale and exhale right now. Remember, only if you can, because if you can do that, you need to praise the Lord! Just when you thought you were the only one going through something, just when you thought your issues were the worst that has ever happened to anyone, just when you thought that your current situation was going to take you under, your praise actually set you apart from your situation. Even if it was for a moment, it was enough time for God to let you know that you will make it! Just think, even with the worst that you may be dealing with, if it was possible, those who are currently hooked to respirators and clinging to life would love to switch places with you! We need to stop complaining so much and praise the Lord. We need to stop doubting so much and just praise the Lord. We need to stop looking at our current situation and praise God that He will bring us to a better situation.

Let me give you an example of what I'm saying. One day,

a young lady told me that her father was in the hospital and she was very tired because she was visiting him around the clock. She was complaining about losing sleep because she was at the hospital so much. She was complaining that her father couldn't walk, but he could only talk at certain times of her visit. Here's what I said to her. I said, "I hear you, but I truly wish I was in your shoes and was able to visit my father." She looked at me and said, "Why don't you?" I told her I couldn't because my father passed away in July 1999.

Do you see my point? Instead of complaining about having to visit her father, she should have praised the LORD that her father is still alive. We need to start praising the LORD until it hurts! With praise comes trust. Because no matter what's going on in your life, you can still find the strength to praise the LORD that will show God that you trust Him with your very life. But if you just complain and complain about what's going on, then that shows that you don't trust God and that you would rather fail than prosper. Keep smiling! Keep believing and know that you're not the only one dealing with something, but with your praise, you will come through!

THOUGHT OF THE DAY

"IT'S COMING TO A THEATRE NEAR YOU, SO WAIT!"

Remember when you were young and you went to an event with your parents and you were excited the entire ride. You didn't care if it was the amusement park, the movies, Chucky Cheese, an arcade arena, etc. All you talked about in the car was how you couldn't wait to get there. Once you arrived, you hopped out of the car and ran to the front gate or door and your parents yelled, "Wait!" They told you to wait because you couldn't get in without them paying for you and you needed adult supervision. Well, this is what the LORD is telling us. We know our season is coming. We can taste it. We can smell it. We can feel it, and because we've gotten a glimpse, we sometimes get overly excited and try to get it on our own in our timing. This is when we need to wait! Wait on the LORD. We need

His supervision, and because He paid the price for us to enter, we should wait on Him to guide us into our season. Trust in the LORD with all your heart!

Scripture of the Day:

> Wait on the LORD; Be of good courage, And He shall strengthen your heart; Wait, I say, on the LORD!
>
> Psalm 27:14 (NKJV)

Don't allow temptation and impatience to mess you up. We often become anxious while waiting and this leads to a lack of faith. With patience comes faith and with faith comes a relationship with God. We need to wait on the LORD and allow Him to do what He has to do to deliver us to our season. You must understand that you are the only person who can mess up what God has for you. The enemy cannot do anything once you make up in your mind that no matter what you are going through, you're going to wait on the LORD.

When finances look dim, wait! When your relationship with your spouse or children seems to be fading, wait! When your job is talking about layoffs, wait! When your position at your job seems to be going nowhere, wait! When your bills are overdue and you've been paying your tithes and offerings, wait! If you don't have a job and you need one, wait! When you were overlooked for that promotion, wait! When you were called to ministry and you couldn't wait to start preaching, wait! You must understand that everything happens in God's order. And with order comes patience. In order for you to be blessed, you must first be able to wait on the LORD to bring you through whatever it is you're going through. Don't allow your impatience keep you up from what you are destined to receive.

THOUGHT OF THE DAY
"AND YOU THOUGHT
IT WAS LUCK!"

On this day, let us be thankful for grace and mercy. Let us praise the LORD, for what was meant for evil, God turned it around and blessed us. That very thing that was meant to destroy you, that very thing that was meant to have you in depression, that very thing that was meant to hinder you and slow you down, God granted grace and mercy over your life and you were not touched at all. What you must remember is God is trying to mold you into the person who will be able to handle the next level in which He is bringing you. If you want to be truly blessed but can't handle what's going on now with the haters and people who mean you no good, then you definitely will not be able to handle what's ahead at the next level. Just keep praising while going through and stay under the covering of the LORD. Many will fall, but you will not be moved. Many will fail, but you will succeed. Many will give up, but the hope of the LORD is on your side. Don't stop praising Him. If the LORD brings you to it, then He will get you through it!

Scripture of the Day:

A thousand may fall at your side, And ten thousand at your right hand; But it shall not come near you.

Psalm 91:7 (NKJV)

And you thought it was luck! You thought it was a coincidence that the eighteen- wheeler just missed you on the highway. You thought when they called for layoffs that it was an error that your name wasn't on the list. Listen, God has a plan for your life. This is why many are falling at your side and many at your right hand, but you still seem to make it out. The great Houdini is not the only escape artist. God is an escape artist, and as long as you keep praising Him, He will keep making a way of escape for you out of what seemed like something that would take you out. You continue to keep wondering how bills are being paid and how you are still able to feed yourself and your family. You keep wondering how so many who make more money than you and live in a bigger home and drive a bigger car seem to not be as happy as you. You have the secret weapon on your side. Because you trusted in the LORD, He granted you favor. He granted you grace and mercy which shall endure in your life forever. Just continue to keep praising the LORD and remember this: for every setback, there's a setup. Somebody just got set free with that. Thank you, LORD!

THOUGHT OF THE DAY
"YOU'VE FALLEN, NOW DUST YOURSELF OFF AND GET BACK UP!"

We have all fallen short of the glory of the LORD. We have all made mistakes in our lives and will continue to make mistakes because there is only one perfect man and His name is Jesus! We know this and understand this, so this is not really the issue. The issue is folks judging us when we do make mistakes. People will do such things and point the finger at you. They will play the blame game with you and they will point the finger, even more so if you are a believer in Christ. I'm sure you've heard before, "Wow, look at what he/she has done and they go to church." Just because you give your life to Christ doesn't make you perfect. Don't allow those folks who do this to discourage you. That is their main purpose, and most of the time they point the finger so they won't have to point the finger at themselves! We just have to learn to come to God with our errors and ask for forgiveness and move on. Don't dwell on them and don't allow people who point the finger at you to make you feel guilty. God will forgive you as soon as you bring it to Him and ask for forgiveness. Just trust in Him!

Scripture of the Day:

> For a righteous man may fall seven times And rise again, but the wicked shall fall by calamity.
> Proverbs 24:16 (NKJV)

Listen. God already knows you are not perfect. He created you, remember? He knows your flaws. He knows your weaknesses. He knows everything. When you allow people to discourage you because of what you have done, God already knows anyhow, then you are cutting your life short. Live your life to the fullest. If you commit a sin or make a mistake, then just bring it to God and ask Him for forgiveness. And what I love about the LORD is you can bring your issue to Him and He will turn you around and around and around if He has to. What the devil meant for evil, God turned it around for the good. Remember, when people point their finger at you, they have four fingers pointing back at themselves. Let them do what they do best and that's try to put the spotlight on you. When they point their finger at you about something you have done, it could be confirmation that the LORD is about to bless you. Remember, God will use those who hate you to bless you. Keep believing!

THOUGHT OF THE DAY
"SCRIPTURE OF THE MONTH: GET YOURS IN THIS YEAR AND DON'T WORRY ABOUT THE HATERS!"

Each day of this month will seem like a challenge to you. Each day will seem like you just need to give up. Each day will seem like your troubles are bigger than God, but I'm here to tell you that your journey has already been won for you. The victory is yours. You just need to endure this season and claim your real season. Just take the blows and the hits and continue on. The mission of the enemy is to only try and make you think that you will not win, but you have already won. The reason why your situations and circumstances seem to be so rough at this point is because somehow, the enemy has tapped into your future. He has peeked in and seen what God is about to do with you, so he's throwing everything at you, including the kitchen sink. Hold on and use what the enemy has seen as strength to continue on.

Scripture of the Day:

'No weapon formed against you shall prosper, And every tongue which rises against you in judgment you shall condemn. This is the heritage of the servants of the LORD, And their righteousness is from Me," Says the LORD.

Isaiah 54:17 (NKJV)

Listen. The weapon will be formed. The haters will hate. Your enemies will do whatever they can to hinder you, but they shall not prosper! All the lies and all the gossip about you in judgment shall not be able to penetrate you! God has got you covered. Receive His Word and walk into your destiny!

THOUGHT OF THE DAY
"THE JOB IS TRYING TO BLESS YOU, BUT YOU KEEP MOVING!"

Let us be thankful for this day knowing that we are that much closer to our breakthrough. We must stay immovable and steadfast in the LORD and know that the work we do is not in vain. The LORD is storing up some stuff for us for the labor we do. I am guilty of this. Stop complaining about the job you do and just do the best you can. The LORD is trying to bless you, but with every complaint, you are hindering yourself from your blessing. If your boss is asking too much of you, if you are being pulled in all directions at work, if you feel like you're doing more than one job, if you feel like you are doing more than those above, if you are working longer hours than you are paid for, this is not the time to complain about it. I know it's tough to remain quiet, but God is using this opportunity to get a blessing out of your labor. If you can just stay immovable in Him and trust in Him, He has something for you.

Scripture of the Day:

> Therefore, my beloved brethren, be steadfast, immovable, always abounding in the work of the LORD, knowing that your labor is not in vain in the LORD.
>
> 1 Corinthians 15:58 (NKJV)

I know some of you may disagree with this, but you should treat the job you have right now as if the LORD Himself is sitting at the cubicle where your boss is sitting. In other words, you should work as if the LORD is your supervisor. If that were the case, would you be taking longer breaks than told to? Would you be taking that extra long lunch break? Would you just complain all day about how much you hate the job? You should be grateful to even have a job with the way the job market is now. Also, if you complain about what the LORD is actually trying to do with you, then you are slowing down your breakthrough. You have to be able to walk in there and say, "No weapon formed against me today by my coworkers or boss shall prosper." You have to be able to walk in there and overlook the chaos and just do what you are asked to do, without complaining.

Let me share this. I remember my supervisor asked me to do these little projects and take on more than I was getting paid for. I was doing the job of a supervisor's assistant but I was still doing my regular job. At first, I must admit, I complained a bit, but then I felt that the LORD was trying to bless me. I went with it and did what I was asked to do. I was actually doing the job of a supervisor's assistant. Then the actual job was posted, my supervisor came to me and told me to apply. I applied and not only did I get the job, but I was compensated extra for it! You never know what the LORD may be trying to do for you at your job. In order to see what He has, you must continue to praise Him in spite of what's going on in the workplace. Stay immovable and know that your work is not in vain. Trust Him!

"BE CAREFUL WITH WHAT YOU CALL A BLESSING!"

Oftentimes, there are people who receive things and say it is from God. Well, for your information, if you swindle to get things, if you cheat on your taxes and get more money and say it's from God, if you get that promotion at work because you lied on the internal application, if you give someone money and tell them it's a gift and as soon as you are down to your last you have the nerve to ask for the money back and you get the money and say, "God is right on time," then you are fooling yourself if you think that's a blessing. God's gift is perfect. Now, that doesn't mean that God will not bless you through those who mean you no good, but the gift will be perfected by the time it gets to you. You, yourself, can get the unworthy one to receive the gift. What I mean is you can't rob a bank and say that God has blessed you with money. We just need to be patient and wait on the Lord's perfect gift because the difference between what the Lord has and what people have is this: what God gives you will never end!

Scripture of the Day:

> Do not be deceived, my beloved brethren. Every good gift and every perfect gift is from above, and comes down from the Father of lights, with whom there is no variation or shadow of turning.
>
> James 1:16–17 (NKJV)

That's where we get messed up. We try and get the blessing before God wants us to get it. Then, we go out and do things we shouldn't be doing, and even if we do receive something from what we did, we then try and give God the credit. No, that's not of God. You are only deceiving yourself. And when you get these things, trust me, they won't last long. But if you can hold out, if you can trust in the Lord, if you can be patient with what God has for you, then that which seemed to be temporary will become permanent. You may think that God has forgotten you because of your current situations, but if you can just look towards the hills from where your help comes from and seek God and praise Him instead of your current situation, God may not come when you want, but He's never late! He may not bless you when you want to be blessed, but you will never receive a blessing after the fact. Just hold onto His word and stay focused on Christ and not what's happening with you or

OUT OF DEATH COMES LIFE

around you. Just take a look out the window … the storm is clearing up in your life!

THOUGHT OF THE DAY
"REGARDLESS OF WHAT YOU'VE DONE, YOU'RE COVERED!"

Oftentimes we say, "T.G.I.F.," which stands for "thank God it's Friday." When I say, "T.G.I.F.," I am saying thank God I'm forgiven! You all should be glad this morning that the LORD looked over your faults and still blessed you today with life. Is there anyone who's glad that your failures weren't fatal? There are many who failed at the same things you failed at, but they are not here to tell it. You are still here. That's enough right there to praise Him all day long. He did not have to do this, but His love, with His grace and mercy, touched us this morning and woke us up. We have the use of our limbs, we have eyesight, we can hear and get around on our own, and even if you have an impairment of some kind, know that the LORD still has blessed you.

We need to thank God that He has forgotten all that we

have done in the past that was not of God, and that He has helped us stay on the path of righteousness. We often beat ourselves up over things we've done, thinking that the LORD will not forgive us but most importantly, thinking that we cannot forgive ourselves! Try the LORD with all the things you have done that you think the LORD will not forgive you for. Keep believing and do not allow the enemy to make you think that you cannot be forgiven. The blood of Christ is already working in your favor. When Christ gave His life for us, He also gave His life so that we may be forgiven of our sins. It's already done. Just bring it to the LORD and let Him wash you clean.

Scripture of the Day:

> I, even I, am He who blots out your transgressions for My own sake; And I will not remember your sins. Put Me in remembrance; Let us contend together; State your case, that you may be acquitted.
>
> Isaiah 43:25–26 (NKJV)

Aren't you glad that God is not like people? You know how we do sometimes when someone does something to us. We say we forgive them, but as soon as something else comes up, we bring up what they've done to us in the past. The LORD will not do this! Once you've sinned against the Father and you bring it to Him asking for forgiveness, for His own sake, He will forget what you have done and cast it away into the sea of forgiveness. State your case. Bring it to Him and He will forgive and forget, but the key is you need to forgive and forget yourself. The enemy will creep up time after time, trying to make you think that God will not forgive you and that you should not forgive yourself because what you may have done was so harsh. The word says God will blot out your transgressions. He did not say He will forgive you of only certain things you may have done. It says He will not remember your sins, no matter what they may be. Trust in Him!

THOUGHT OF THE DAY
"OT IS NEEDED FOR YOUR BREAKTHROUGH!"

Who works overtime at their job? Overtime is when you work more hours than you are normally expected to work, and for those extra hours, you are usually paid time and a half. Some people may be salary, but when you work extra hours, you are given compensation for the extra time worked. Now my question is who has "OT Praise?" Who wants to be compensated extra for their extra praise? Here's what's considered OT praise: when you've done all you can and your situation still seems to be consuming you, but you put in that extra time to praise God! When your bank account is negative and you are waiting for that paycheck and until then you are flat broke, but you still put in that extra time to praise God. When people mean you no good and those people were once your closest friends, but you still have time to praise God! Listen. All these things and much more may be happening in your life, but the LORD wants you to know that it shall come to pass. What you have to do is put in that OT praise and don't allow your situation to distract your praise.

Scripture of the Day:

I, the LORD, have spoken it; It shall come to pass, and I will do it.

Ezekiel 24:14a (NKJV)

Start praising right now for what the LORD has already done. You may not see it, but it shall come to pass. You may not feel it, but it shall come to pass. You may not smell it, but it shall come to pass. You know how when you're going home after work and before you get to the door you can smell the food cooking and all of a sudden your stomach feels funny and you instantly get hungry and can't wait to eat? Well, in the spirit, you may be that close to your breakthrough. The aroma has hit your nostrils and you started to feel funny inside and you just can't wait to get to it. You can't see the aroma, you can't feel it in the natural, but you can smell it. With the smell comes faith that it shall come to pass. Just take a whiff today and understand that the LORD said He will do it! Put in that extra time to praise Him. Put in that extra time to worship Him.

Stop having pity parties because when you have pity parties, I hope you've noticed, only the haters want to party with you. When the believers hear about you having a pity party, they don't want to attend because attending the party only encourages you to stay in pity. Their absence should let you know that God has something better for you. Believers will pray for you instead. You will not see them pray, you may not hear them pray, but if you can take a whiff of the aroma of what God is doing through their prayer for you, you will blow out those candles and put in that OT for God!

THOUGHT OF THE DAY
"GET A NEW PRAISE
FOR THIS NEW DAY
AND BE SET FREE!"

Let us rejoice today and understand that God has granted us new life. Not only did He grant us life, but He has granted us new life on this day. Each day we arise, we are granted new life from our God. Yesterday has passed away, but you haven't. You need to get a new praise going. You need to get new prayers going. You need to worship the LORD in a new way. The situations you faced yesterday may still be here today but because you have new life; because you have new mercies; you will be able to face the situations with a fresh spirit. It is up to you. God has already placed it before you. Just receive it! Don't allow your situation to make you think that God has forgotten you, because the truth of the matter is if God had forgotten about you, you would not be reading this. New mercies were given to you this morning!

_____

Scripture of the Day:

> Through the LORD's mercies we are not consumed, Because His compassions fail not. They are new every morning; Great is Your faithfulness. 'The LORD is my portion,' says my soul,' Therefore I hope in Him.'
>
> Lamentations 3:22–24 (NKJV)

Thank God for having mercy on us. With all that goes on in our lives everyday, with all we've done in the past, with all we do now, God still loves us enough to grant us new mercies each day! Because of His new mercy, we should have a new praise for Him. Keep your hope in Him and not in man. Stop believing the world and believe God! Just because the stock market is falling and jobs seem to be unavailable and the economy is going down and terrorism is on the rise and violence is amongst us and our debt seems to be overtaking us … with each day you're given new mercy and with that new mercy you should have hope in Him. Get a praise going right now as you read this and start to free yourself from yourself! Out of all the things in life that could hold you back, you could be holding yourself back. Get a new praise for His new mercy.

"I FEEL LIKE DANCING. DO YOU?"

This is the day that the LORD has made. I'm not going to worry about tomorrow or think of yesterday, but I'm going to praise the LORD today. And during my praise I'm going to give Him a dance. Listen, don't stop now; don't give in now, for this is your season. You can acknowledge to the LORD that it's your season by giving Him a dance! God is changing situations right now. God is turning things around in your life, and if you can continue to praise Him, if you can continue to worship Him, if you can continue to labor for Him even in the midst of your troubles, if you can continue to dance for Him, He will keep His promise to you!

The only person who can stop God from blessing you is you! Your haters can't stop you. Those bills can't stop you. Your job can't stop you. Your boss can't stop you. Once God puts His hand on you, only you can release yourself. Because of this, you ought to give Him a dance this morning. But know this: whenever you start to give God glory, whenever you start to dance before the LORD, somebody is not going to like it! But listen. Can you stand to be blessed? Let them hate, let them dislike it. They don't know where God has brought you from, so just dance, dance, dance, dance … for the LORD today!

Scripture of the Day:

> Then David danced before the LORD with all his might; and David was wearing a linen ephod. So David and all the house of Israel brought up the ark of the LORD with shouting and with the sound of the trumpet. Now as the ark of the LORD came into the City of David, Michal, Saul's daughter, looked through a window and saw King David leaping and whirling before the LORD; and she despised him in her heart.
>
> 2 Samuel 6:14–16 (NKJV)

You see, David was facing some challenges in his life and God brought him through, so David started to acknowledge the LORD with a dance. He didn't care who was around. He didn't care what folks said. He made as much noise as possible and not only did he dance, but he danced with all his might! Let me throw this in here: are you praising the LORD with all your might? It could be the reason why you are still in the midst of your troubles, because you continue to give Him half praise! You have to praise Him and do it as if it's going to be your last praise!

Also, as you can see when David danced for the LORD, people didn't like it and hated him for it. Never mind who's watching you, never mind who's going to hate you, never mind if you look foolish, they don't know what God has done for you. You may have been headed for destruction and God spared your life, so praise Him! You had all kinds of bills and they were more than your paycheck but somehow He made a way out of no way, so praise Him! You were unemployed and a job was just thrown at you, so praise Him! Get your groove on this morning. Get your dance on this morning. Let the God that has brought you out know that you acknowledge Him and will continue to acknowledge Him, regardless of who's watching or hating. Dance with all your might!

"PART I—WHO NEEDS TO GO ON A SPIRITUAL DIET?"

Who needs to lose weight today? Before anyone gets offended, what I mean is spiritual weight. To lose this type of weight, you don't need workout tapes, you don't need the stair master, and you don't need to be a member at your local gym ... all you need is to trust in the LORD! What is spiritual weight? I'm glad you asked. It's when someone offends you and you carry that grudge on your shoulders while the person who offended you is doing all right. It's when you have that burden and, for some strange reason, you won't let it go. It's when you have so much on your mind that you can't be the person God destined you to be. All of this will eventually start to weigh you down. What you need to do is trust in the LORD that He will take care of everything that is weighing you down. When you are burdened, your praise isn't the same. When you are burdened, your worship isn't the same. What you need to do is lose that weight so you can be light on your feet. You need to lose that weight so your mind can be free. Trust in the LORD and He will remove everything that was meant to weigh you down.

Scripture of the Day:

It shall come to pass in that day That his burden will be taken away from your shoulder, And his yoke from your neck, And the yoke will be destroyed because of the anointing oil.

Isaiah 10:27 (NKJV)

It's already been spoken! Everything that you are carrying that you shouldn't be carrying will be taken from you. The day will come to pass. You must keep praising the LORD. Continue to worship the LORD. Don't allow the things that are trying to weigh you down consume you. Know that whatever it is that is weighing you down shall be removed from your shoulders. The yoke shall be destroyed. Keep your focus on the LORD and what He has for you.

I understand that some issues and problems are very intense, but if you can trust that the LORD will bring you out and start living as if you are already out of that situation, then you will be in a better place mentally! This is where the battle field truly is … in your mind. This is what the enemy will use to fight against you. If he can get in your mind and make you think that you will fail, if he can make you think that God will not deliver you from whatever is weighing you down, if he can make you think that you are wasting your time praising and worshiping the LORD, then he has you right where he wants you to be. Frustration will then set in. Misery will then set in. Anger will then set in, and much more. But you have to trust the LORD enough to know that He will, and already has, delivered you from that situation. Get your exercise on but this type of exercise does not require any video tapes or treadmills. It only requires that you trust in the LORD and praise and worship. Stand up right now! I don't care where you are when you read this. Just thank the LORD for what He is about to do in your life. Try it!

THOUGHT OF THE DAY
"PART II—LOSE THAT SPIRITUAL WEIGHT!"

Remember when that person offended you? Remember when that person irked your last nerve? Remember when that person did something to you and you just thought that you would never forgive them? Well I hope you can forgive them for whatever it was they have done. If you hold that grudge and don't let go of it by forgiving them, then you are setting yourself up for a miserable life until you let it go. When you do not forgive, you are letting God know that you don't want Him to forgive you from the wrong you have done. It doesn't matter who did it, or what they did. You need to let it go. Now, don't get me wrong, it doesn't mean you have to still interact with this person. The Word doesn't say that. The Word says to forgive them and have that burden lifted from your shoulders, because one day it will be your turn to have your track record reviewed and if you haven't forgiven them, then you won't be forgiven! Trust the LORD.

Scripture of the Day:

> For if you forgive men their trespasses, your heavenly Father will also forgive you. But if you do not forgive men their trespasses, neither will your Father forgive your trespasses.
>
> Matthew 6:14–15 (NKJV)

Many times, we carry extra baggage around with us. Instead of us letting things go, we subconsciously tell ourselves that we will never forgive people for what they did. Here's what happens: your subconscious will eat at you day after day until you let it go. I do understand that there are some devious things that may have been done to you, but it's up to you to learn to forgive them for what they have done and allow the LORD to handle it. You need to let it go! Also, if there were times when you messed up with someone and you hurt their feelings. When you go to the LORD asking for forgiveness, the LORD will remind you of when you didn't forgive that person for what they did to you. Today is part II of losing spiritual weight. This time the excess baggage is those burdens you carry when you refuse to forgive those individuals who offended you in some type of way. At some point today, take a moment to pray about this and just let it go. The LORD has been waiting for you to let it go so He can deal with it. Give Him a chance!

THOUGHT OF THE DAY
"PART III—YOU DON'T NEED A PILL TO LOSE THIS WEIGHT!"

You don't need a pill to lose spiritual weight, all you need is praise! Many of you may be that much closer to your breakthrough today, but what's holding you back is that sin which is burdening you. Every time you try to praise Him, here comes that issue. Every time you try to worship Him, here comes that issue. Every time you try to seek Him or spend time with Him, here comes that issue. You must understand that the enemy is using you to stop you! Because the very thing that is holding you back, the very thing that is resting on your shoulders, the very thing that is burdening you is actually being held on to by you. Did you know that *we* chose not to let go of 99.9 percent of our issues? God will not force you to let go. You must choose to let it go. Lay aside every weight and once you choose to do this, you will be lighter on your feet. Then you will be able to reach higher and higher because that extra weight that was holding you down will be gone. Reach up to the LORD and grab hold of His promises!

Scripture of the Day:

> Therefore we also, since we are surrounded by so great a cloud of witnesses, let us lay aside every weight, and the sin which so easily ensnares us, and let us run with endurance the race that is set before us, looking unto Jesus, the author and finisher of our faith, who for the joy that was set before Him endured the cross, despising the shame, and has sat down at the right hand of the throne of God.
>
> Hebrews 12:1–2 (NKJV)

Have you noticed in the natural that all the fastest runners in the world, all the runners who had the most endurance, were all light on their feet? It seemed the heavier they were, the slower they were, and they often couldn't finish the race due to lack of endurance. In the spiritual realm, if we are carrying too much, if we are overburdened, if we are insincere with our praise and worship then we are losing the race. For Christ suffered for us, not to lose the race, but to win the race. And because He wrote the blueprint of our race, and because He also finished the race for us, then we cannot fail unless we choose to. Let's get in spiritual shape! Let's become light on our feet so that we are able to praise the LORD with energy in spite of what may be going on in our lives today. Start praising Him! Start worshiping Him and watch the weight start to fall off in the name of Jesus. Trust in Him!

THOUGHT OF THE DAY
"YOU ARE WHAT YOU SPEAK!"

I know you all know the old saying, "You are what you eat." Well, I also want you to know that you are what you speak! Oftentimes we go through things and God is trying to deliver us from what we are going through, but sometimes He can't. I know you're probably saying, "How can God not deliver us from something?" Well it's true. Christ could not perform some miracles in His hometown because the people in the town did not believe He could do so. They also spoke death in their own lives.

The same applies today. If you are one who complains and just nags, you're negative about everything, you continue to speak failure and poverty into your life and you speak that layoffs will affect your department and that you are not worthy of what God has for you, then you are actually speaking death into your life. You may not be physically dying, but your dreams and blessings will die because of what you are speaking. This is why you have to be very careful how you criticize yourself. If you want to be delivered from what you are currently facing, then you need to start speaking that it's already done. Start having faith in what God is doing in your life. It may not seem so to you now, but He is allowing that very thing that is going on to bless you. Speak blessings today!

Scripture of the Day:

> Death and life are in the power of the tongue,
> And those who love it will eat its fruit.
> Proverbs 18:21 (NKJV)

You have the power! You are the one who can have deliverance brought into your life. God is trying to do so but you are holding Him back! Allow your faith to hook up with what God is doing and be set free. Be set free from debt. Be set free from that addiction. Be set free from people. But before that you can be set free, you have to believe that God can do it, and one of the ways to show belief is to speak it. God can't deliver you from that situation if you don't believe He can. Start speaking victory today. Start speaking prosperity. Start speaking promotions. Start speaking the LORD in your life. Don't allow those around you to lure you into their negativity. If they choose to be negative about what's going on around them, let them, but you keep a yes and an amen in your spirit. Don't allow what you see affect where God is trying to take you because where He's trying to take you right now is unseen. Remember, if you can speak it, then you'll be it!

THOUGHT OF THE DAY
"LOOK UP IN THE SKY. IT'S A BIRD. NO, IT'S A PLANE. NO, IT'S JESUS!"

Let's be thankful on this day because this is the day that the LORD has made for you and me. Let us rejoice and be glad in it. The LORD sent His angels to watch over us throughout the night. Let us praise Him for our troubles that are both seen and unseen. What do I mean by unseen? The LORD kept you from that car accident that you didn't know about. You didn't hear it last night, but the death angel came for you and the LORD answered on your behalf. You didn't hear it last night, but cancer knocked on your door for you and the LORD answered it on your behalf. You see, we often take for granted the stuff we don't see, but we must understand that the LORD is watching over us and is our help in times of trouble. Because you are alive today, does it really matter you don't have that job you wanted? Does it matter that you don't have that outfit you wanted? Here's the problem, we tend to put more time and effort into changing those things instead of seeking God in our troubles! If you were to seek Him first, then all those things would turn around. Get that 360 degree praise going because you want the LORD to turn some things around for you.

Scripture of the Day:

God is our refuge and strength, A very present help in trouble.

Psalm 46:1 (NKJV)

Call upon Me in the day of trouble; I will deliver you, and you shall glorify Me.

Psalm 50:15 (NKJV)

These scriptures go hand in hand. I want you to underline the word *present*. I am truly convinced that we are living in the last days. There's so much going on in this country and the world that is making it more obvious that we are living in the last days. I truly believe that the LORD is fed up with us as a people and He is allowing all this to happen. However, for the believers He is still a present help in times of trouble. All you have to do is call on Him and He will deliver you from that very situation. God has the divine total phone, so you will never get a busy signal when you call on Him! He won't look at the caller ID and not answer. Just call on Him and He will deliver. He is where our strength comes from. He is where our help comes from. What you must understand is even before that trouble hit your household or your workplace, God was already there.

Okay, back to the word *present*. As you read, it says, "He's a very present help in times of trouble." There are two meanings to that word as used in this scripture. First, the word *present* means that while your troubles are happening, He's right there to provide a way of escape. He is present! Also, the word *present* means gifts! Okay, what are you saying Troy? Not only will God be right there in your troubles, but while in your troubles, He's storing up gifts for you. While in those troubles, just keep praise. While facing those troubles, continue to worship Him and watch Him deliver you and also bless you at the same time. Give Him praise right now. That very issue you have today is only to bless you. That setback has really set you up for something!

"DO YOU HAVE P.M.S. TODAY?"
(PRAISE FOR A MOMENT SYNDROME)

Today PMS stands for, **P**raise for a **M**oment **S**yndrome! As you all know, a woman's body goes through a cycle once a month to cleanse out her body. During this time, the woman usually has cramps and feels a bit down and is sometimes moody. Well, let the truth be known, men may not go through the monthly body cleansing, but we do have PMS often. We do get moody from time to time, so women, you're not alone. That's as close as I can get to the biological meaning of PMS. The point of this is to set a foundation for where I'm trying to go. The woman deals with this once a month, usually during the same time of month when she's on a regular cycle. Then at some point in life, the woman's body changes and then she faces menopause. At this point, the cycle of PMS has stopped!

Okay, follow me. In the spiritual we are usually faced with situations and circumstances in our lives, whether it is dealing with people who you know dislike you, overdue bills, a rocky divorce, hard-headed children, or layoffs or anything burdening you right now; these issues usually make us have PMS! You see, we can only praise for a moment. We can only give God the glory when things are going well. Once a month when everything is going well, then we praise the LORD, instead of praising each and every day. The word says when the praises go up, the blessings come down. If you only can praise Him once a month because you are moody and crampy and you have issues, then you are telling Him that you don't trust Him enough to get you out of that situation. You can only praise Him once a month. You can only praise Him when things seem to be all right. You need to get rid of that PMS. You need divine menopause in your life. In other words, you need the Praise for a Moment Syndrome to stop and then begin to praise Him all day, every day! Trust in the LORD!

Scripture of the Day:

Every day I will bless You, And I will praise Your name forever and ever.

Psalm 145:2 (NKJV)

Praise the LORD! Praise the LORD, O my soul!
While I live I will praise the LORD; I will sing
praises to my God while I have my being.

Psalm 146:1–2 (NKJV)

There's a pattern here. If you read those scriptures again, you will see that it's not saying to praise Him when things are going well. It's not saying to praise Him only when you get that promotion, or when you receive that income tax check, or when you get married … it says to praise Him with all your soul forever! As long as you have breath this morning, you should be praising Him. Regardless of what you are facing today, let the LORD know that you trust in Him and you will praise Him forever and ever! He has already given you peace over that circumstance. No more PMS–no more Praising Him for a Moment Syndrome! It's time to praise the LORD and know that your **revelation** is bigger than your **situation**!

THOUGHT OF THE DAY
"DON'T RUN FROM YOUR BLESSING, JUST SIT AT THE TABLE AND GET FED!"

Today I had something that I wanted to share with you, but I was led by the Holy Spirit to share this instead. The LORD is trying to bless you tremendously! Oftentimes He will use our enemies to bless us, but because we recognize them as enemies, we won't allow this to happen. Just receive it! It truly doesn't matter who blesses you, just realize that it's from God. You've been praying for a while now. You've been fasting, you've been faithful, you've come so far, and you mean to tell me, that if the LORD uses your enemy to bless you, you wouldn't want to be bothered? This may be the last time this blessing comes forth, and with the pride that we have sometimes…you know how we do. We'll say things like, "Oh, I know he/she don't like me, I'm not taking anything from them. I'd rather wait until the LORD sends someone I like to bless me. I don't need what they have for me because I know they aren't sincere in their giving." Listen, people of God, you better just receive it and move on. God will use whoever and whatever He wants to bless His children. Just be patient and receive.

Scripture of the Day:

You prepare a table before me in the presence of my enemies; You anoint my head with oil; My cup runs over.

Psalm 23:5 (NKJV)

You haven't received your blessing because your table is not complete. All those who need to be there to see you get blessed have not been put in place. The LORD wants to bless you and have all those who lied on you, set traps for you, gossiped about you, hated on you, tried to talk about you to others to make them dislike you, those who actually prayed against you, those who even stole from you ... God wants all those folks at the table when you receive your blessing. You must have the Spirit of God upon you in order to put them in place. You have to be able to walk in their midst and not be intimidated. You need to be able to work with them at your job and get the job done effectively. You need to be able to see them in church and embrace them with true love. When you can do this, the LORD will place them at your table. You may be two hugs away from your breakthrough! Don't run to someone you like to hug, don't run to someone you like to work with, head right for those who mean you no good and let the Spirit of the LORD reign over them.

Here's a commercial break; you may just be the only God they know! Let them get delivered through you!

THOUGHT OF THE DAY
"OKAY, IT'S YOUR CHOICE. NOW WHAT?"

Choices! That's what life is all about. I must admit, when I came to the LORD and received Him in my heart, the first thing I wanted to do was to try and make as many people come to Christ as possible. When I didn't get the results I wanted, I felt as if God was not a part of my life anymore, but now I truly know that life is about choices and that choosing God is a personal choice. The reality of the situation is you can preach the Gospel to folks until they turn green, but when they come to that fork in the road - one road is life with Christ, the other is destruction with the enemy - some people are still going to choose destruction! It's sad, but true. This is why I choose to do what I do in Christ, and I don't try and force it on anyone. It's your choice. I will still love you the same.

Scripture of the Day:

> Therefore, if anyone is in Christ, he is a new creation; old things have passed away; behold, all things have become new.
>
> 2 Corinthians 5:17 (NKJV)

Now, as I said before, life is about choices. If you choose Christ, then the old things will pass away. This is a daily process of living with Christ. It won't just be a 'poof-poof' and all of a sudden you have no issues. No, it will be daily, but know at least you will have the upper hand. You will be delivered from all of the issues you used to have if you allow Christ to handle it. Your life will be renewed. Your finances will be renewed. Your relationships with people will be renewed. Your health will be renewed. All these things, and more, will be renewed. You just have to give Christ a chance.

I am asking all of you to share this word with someone today. Read it to them and or let them read it. Send this word to those who you think need to hear the good word of the LORD. Send it to those who are going through some stuff and may not believe in God or may not believe what He can do. Share this with those who you know feel like giving up on life because of the hand they were dealt. Share this with those who are experiencing depression in their life because of their current situation. Let this be shared throughout the world because the bottom line is, sooner or later you'll know who's greater! It will either be Christ or the crises.

THOUGHT OF THE DAY
"WHAT THE DEVIL MEANT FOR EVIL, GOD TURNED IT AROUND!"

This is the day! This is the day you receive your blessing. This is the day you receive what God has for you. Just start praise that will make the LORD have no choice but to bless you. Sometimes when we praise the LORD, we are not sincere with our praise and God does not take us seriously, so He just moves on with His blessings. You have to truly get the LORD's attention. This is one of the reasons why you haven't obtained what He has for you—because you haven't gotten His attention. And when you don't get God's attention, you then get the attention of the enemy. Here's what I've come to learn: people only go through things because somehow the enemy has seen a bit of their future! He has seen what God has for you and his job is to steal, kill, and destroy your life and your dreams because he wants to stop you. The only one who can stop you, is you!

Scripture of the Day:

> The thief does not come except to steal, and to kill, and to destroy. I have come that they may have life, and that they may have it more abundantly.
>
> John 10:10 (NKJV)

It's truly up to you. It's just that simple. Who will you believe? The enemy or Christ? Now, would you trust and believe in someone who's come to kill you, destroy you, and steal all your riches? Or will you trust and believe in someone who died for you, who shed His blood so you can have error in your life and still live; someone who died so you can have freedom; someone who not only gave you life, but gave you a more abundant life? The choice is yours.

Now, things may be happening in your life right now that don't seem like God is working on your behalf. You may be feeling like giving up. You may be feeling like you are on your own and that God has forgotten you, but God is only allowing this to build you. He came that you may have a more abundant life, and in order to receive that, you will have to endure some things. If you can keep praise in your mouth, if you can keep praise in your wallet, if you can keep praise in your church, if you can keep praise within yourself, all the places where it seems like things are going bad... that's where God will bless you. Stay in the game. If necessary, call a timeout to praise God. This will let God know that you can't do it on your own, and that's when He will enter your situation and rearrange some stuff.

THOUGHT OF THE DAY
"WHO WANTS PEACE TO BE STILL FOR A MOMENT?"

Today is a bit different. Before I move on, I'm warning those who read this that you are reading this at your own risk! I want those who have a lot of faith to vibe with me. For those who may not have that much faith, then I pray this will encourage you to a point where your faith will grow. Now if you didn't know, God allows things to happen to us only to help us grow. The enemy cannot do anything to you without permission from God first. When you have those troubles, when you have issues, when problems come into your life, know that the enemy went to God and asked if he could mess with you and God said yes! Here's where your faith should kick in.

You may think that God does not care because He knows about and allowed your current troubles. God uses troubles to make you grow. God uses issues and circumstances to stretch you as a person and to enlarge your faith. When you go through something, you tend to pray harder. You tend to pray and seek God more. Your faith stretches and grows because you feel pushed into a corner. Are you with me so far? That's why God allows issues to come in your life and often will not want you to have peace, because when you have problems, your faith in Him will grow. When you are idle and nothing is going wrong in your life and you are just going from day to day with nothing pushing you, your faith is not maturing because it has nothing to help mature it!

Scripture of the Day:

On the same day, when evening had come, He said to them, 'Let us cross over to the other side.'

And a great windstorm arose, and the waves beat into the boat, so that it was already filling. But He was in the stern, asleep on a pillow. And they awoke Him and said to Him, 'Teacher, do You not care that we are perishing?' Then He arose and rebuked the wind, and said to the sea, 'Peace, be still!' And the wind ceased and there was a great calm. But He said to them, 'Why are you so fearful? How is it that you have no faith?' And they feared exceedingly, and said to one another, 'Who can this be, that even the wind and the sea obey Him!'

Mark 4:35, 37–41 (NKJV)

After reading this and really looking it over, I noticed something. When Jesus first spoke, He already said that they would make it to the other side. He said it, so it didn't matter how the storm raged; it didn't matter how the sea tried to consume them and how the raging waters seemed to be trying to overcome them. Jesus already said that they would make it. No matter what is going on in your life, Jesus already said you would make it. When the storm started raging at its worst, the disciples awoke Jesus from His sleep and asked if He even cared that they were about to perish. Jesus got up and said, "Peace, be still!" Now, after reading this over and over, I noticed something. Jesus actually wanted peace to stop! He wanted those on the boat to have their faith increase by believing that they would get to the other side. There really was no need to awake Him because He already spoke and said they would make it.

That's what God is saying today. Who has enough faith to believe they will make it? You don't actually have to call on Him all the time. If He already spoke to your spirit, if He already promised you something, then your faith should speed up the process rather than asking for your situation to be peaceful. As I said earlier, when there is peace, most of the time your faith can't grow. That's why God commanded the sea to stop raging, and then He asked them this question: "Why are you so fearful? How is it that you have no faith?" Don't pray for peace in your life today. Know that God will not allow you to perish.

Situations may be raging in your life, but God is right there and He has already commanded everything to stop! Now your faith in Him has to catch up. The God I know will not allow you to go under. He has already spoken victory in your life, so stop asking for peace and just let your faith in Him grow. Let your faith in Him be stretched and your territory of faith enlarged. God is awesome and you are made in His image, so you are awesome! Let me tell you what my son told me. My bracelet has the initials W.W.J.D. written on it, which stands for What Would Jesus Do. My son told me that W.W.J.D. also has another meaning if you reverse the letters: Devil Just Won't Win! Now give God praise for slowing down and stopping peace in your life so you can grow in Him!

THOUGHT OF THE DAY
"PRAYER DAY!"

Today is a bit different. I'm usually led to do this from time to time.

Well today, I want us to pray! I'm going to pray through this writing for all the recipients of this writing and your family members. I would like for you to pray for me and my family. I'm facing some challenges and I need *your* prayers to hook up with *my* prayers for myself. This is how I'll start my prayer for you:

Prayer for the Day:

May the LORD give you increase more and more,
You and your children. May you be blessed by
the LORD, Who made heaven and earth.

Psalm 115:14–15 (NKJV)

Let me add to the prayer for you: Lord, most high God, I thank you for my friends. I thank you for those who are reading this who are your servants, Lord God. I thank you for what you've done in their lives and what you're going to do in their lives. If any are sick, heal them. If any are depressed, bring them joy. If any are bound, deliver them. If any need a miracle today, grant them! Most high God, many may be hurting right now, and because of this hurt, it may be slowing them down from praising you. I'm asking that you touch their very lives right now in the name of Jesus and remove that pain so you can be lifted up and glorified!

Lord, we need to hear from you today. There is so much going on around us, we need you to come into our lives today and fill us with your Holy Spirit. Touch not only those reading this but touch their family members also. Lord, I'm asking you to touch the hearts of those family members who may not know you on a personal basis. Bring them to you so they can join in on the everlasting party which will begin once our assignment is done here. Bring about peace in our lives. Lord, bring about deliverance in our lives. Guide us, teach us, mold us, and bless us. Give us guidance today. Give us direction today. Lord, show us the way.

Thank you, Lord, for the blood that has kept us through our errors. Thank you, for giving your only Son so that we are be able to make mistakes and continue on, because we know if you had not done what you did, we would not be able to do what we do! Thank you, in Jesus' name! Bless those who read this book as soon as they open it. Start a transfer in their bank accounts. Do a new thing in their health. Do a new thing in their jobs. Grant them whatever they ask. You said, Lord, that if we ask, we shall receive, and this morning, I'm coming to you with my friends to say we need you right now! Thank you and I give you the praise right now for what you're doing through this book of inspirational writings! In the matchless name of Jesus, we all say amen!

THOUGHT OF THE DAY
"IF HE/SHE COULD ONLY SEE ME NOW ... "

We are dedicating today to our loved ones who have passed on, to those who have been an inspiration to us and loved us unconditionally. I'm sure all of you have lost someone who meant a lot to you and you're at a stage in your life where you wish, "If he/she could only see me now!" Oftentimes I drive around and wish that dad was still here, just so he can see what I have become and where I am going. What is very important about this is the fact we are actually absent. The word says that once we become absent from this body, we will then become present with the Lord. And once we become present with the Lord, then we will become present with those loved ones that passed before us and had a personal relationship with the Lord!

Make sure you stay focused. Make sure that you continue to praise the Lord. Make sure you keep praying, so then you will be able to say, "If he/she could only see me now." There's nothing wrong with missing those who passed away before you and there's nothing wrong with crying, but through those times, you must not let the fact that they are gone consume you. Every time that tear drops from missing them, every time your heart aches, every time you look at something and it reminds you of them, every time you look at a family member that reminds you of them, just look up and say to yourself, "If he/she could only see me now." You've come so far, it's not the time to relapse now. God is moving and will continue to move in your life as long as you can keep the faith in Him!

In remembrance of my dad, Nathaniel Moore, Sr., who became present with the LORD on July 10, 1999! Remember, it's not what you did that makes you present with God, but it's what you believe in your heart!

THOUGHT OF THE DAY
OLD SCHOOL TELEVISION SHOWS—PART 1 "TODAY WE ARE VIEWING DIFFERENT STROKES!"

You all know I'm a bit different. The LORD put this on my heart, so I'll share it with you. Today we are starting with "old school" television shows. I'll be using titles from television shows of the past and relating the TELEVISION show title to the word of God! Today we're looking at *Different Strokes.* I pray you all remember that television show. The characters Arnold and Willis were adopted by a rich family. The title of the show was used because the setup was different. The family unit was different. There were two, inner city, ghetto kids being raised by a rich, upper class family. The kids were peculiar people to this family, but they were loved nonetheless.

Where am I going with this? I'm glad you asked! We have been adopted by the richest of the richest: Christ, Himself! Even though we have been placed in an unstable place called the world, we are in this world, but not of this world. We are here because we are a chosen generation and God has granted us time here to go and get those who are also chosen, but don't realize it as of yet! God has brought us out of darkness into His marvelous light, and we have to get our brothers and sisters! We are different!

Scripture of the Day:

> But you are a chosen generation, a royal priesthood, a holy nation, His own special people, that you may proclaim the praises of Him who called you out of darkness into His marvelous light.
>
> 1 Peter 2:9 (NKJV)

This is why I say I'm different all the time. The Bible declares that we are different. We are peculiar. You should want to be a little strange. It's time to be different. Don't behave the way people expect you to behave. They expect you to complain because you have bills. They expect you to go to the package store because you had a drinking problem. They expect you to give up because you mother/father gave up. They expect you to fail because they see no support around you. They expect you to be in debt because you're a single mom or single dad, but today we declare *different strokes*. In other words, we are going to be the total opposite of what they expect.

You've taken the enemy's best hit, and you're still here! Now give Him praise for being able to praise Him! You could have been locked up, you could have been in the hospital clinging to life, you could be out of your mind this morning, but you're still here! Why? Because God has declared that you are different. Today give Him a different praise! Do not give Him the same praise you gave Him last week!

OLD SCHOOL TELEVISION SHOWS—PART II "TODAY WE ARE VIEWING ONE DAY AT A TIME!"

Today's old school television show is *One Day at a Time*. It was the television show where there were three women, a mother and her two daughters, living together and it was tough for them to make ends meet. It was also tough on the mother who was raising two girls on her own, so she basically just took one day at a time. Well for us, we need to understand that God is still in control. Someone needed to hear that. You're dealing with so much today and all you think about is how you are going to get out of that situation. All you think about is the stress of that situation, but you need to just trust the LORD and take *one day at a time*.

Also, you must understand that the LORD is on His way

back! Whatever it is that God has put on your heart, you need to hurry up and do what God has told you to do. There's no time for you to worry about your issues. Oftentimes, and we are good at this, we'll say, "I'll do that tomorrow." You will tell yourself that you will call your sister or brother tomorrow and they may pass away over night. You will tell yourself that you will pay your tithes next week and the blessing God had for you is not released! You tell yourself that you will give your life to the LORD on Easter Sunday and you don't make it 'til then! It's time to take "One Day at a Time" and do what we have to do for the LORD *today*. Stop putting stuff off for tomorrow, because tomorrow is not promised!

Scripture of the Day:

> Do not boast about *tomorrow*, For you do not know what a day may bring forth.
>
> Proverbs 27:1 (NKJV)

I've said this before and I'll say it again. I know many of you have a list of things you need to do today. You write things down so you won't forget something. This is usually called a "to do list." You may have such things as, pick up dry cleaning, go to grocery store, mail bills out, stop by store after work, etc. But how many of you have on your list: killed in car accident today, sudden heart attack today, get fired from work today, commit suicide today, have a stroke and be paralyzed today? Why don't you have those things on your list? Because you don't expect those things to happen, but in reality they can! We need to start taking day-to-day life more seriously, and if you don't have Christ in your life, this is an excellent time to do so. We don't know what each day will bring. Remember to take "One Day at a Time" and add Christ to your life!

THOUGHT OF THE DAY
OLD SCHOOL TELEVISION SHOWS—PART III "TODAY, WE ARE VIEWING CHEERS!"

Today I have two words for you, **"cheer up!"** The old school television show we will focus on today is *Cheers*. I'm sure you remember this show. It was filmed in a bar, and if you notice, in every show at least one or two of the characters had an issue to deal with. By the time the episode was over, the issue was resolved. That's where our faith should be. We need to know that no matter what we're dealing with, by the time God decides to bring us out, it should be over with. The problem is our faith doesn't think God will ever bring us out.

Let me ask this question (keep it real with your answer): have you ever dealt with an issue for so long that you just started to accept it? You told yourself, "this will never go away." If so, you have just told God that He can't bring you out. You see God can only deliver us according to our faith. Remember the blind man Bartamaeus? His faith made Him well. Remember the woman with the issue of blood? Her faith made her well. Today, cheer up and know that no matter what you're dealing with, God has overcome it already and you're about to come out too! Cheer up, it's done! It's done!

Scripture of the Day:

These things I have spoken to you, that in Me you may have peace. In the world you will have tribulation; but be of good *cheer*, I have overcome the world.

John 16:33 (NKJV)

First, just go ahead and admit to yourself that you have issues. Christ said that in this world you will have issues, but the miracle is that He has overcome everything you're dealing with already. Your faith must catch up so you can be delivered, healed, and set free. Christ has overcome sickness because by His stripes we are healed! Christ has overcome poverty, bills, and financial issues because He emptied Himself out and become poor so that we might be rich! Christ has overcome feeling lonely because He said He would never leave you, nor forsake you! Christ has overcome depression. He said to be of good cheer because in me you will have peace! And no matter what you're dealing with, Christ said, "I have overcome that!" Cheer up today!

Everything you are dealing with is temporary, and it will be over before you know it as long as you have faith.

THOUGHT OF THE DAY
OLD SCHOOL TELEVISION SHOWS—THE CONCLUSION "TODAY, WE ARE VIEWING GOOD TIMES!"

Today is the conclusion of the old school television shows series. We're going to end with *Good Times*! I know you all remember that television show. That was the show with J.J. and Florida Evans, lil' bro Michael Evans, sista Thelma, and the father James Evans. They were a poor family living in the ghetto, but they never gave up on hope. They never gave in. They continued on and on, believing that one day they would move out of the hood! They had dreams and they wouldn't allow them to die. They had faith because they believed that they were living in "Good Times," but they also believed that "Better Times" were coming. Y'all don't hear me! You see we are living in "Good Times." It doesn't matter what's going on in your life. You are blessed. How do I know? I know you are blessed because you are reading this email. You aren't blessed because I'm writing this message. You are blessed because you can read it! You missed that! There are people who would love to take on your issues. Why? Their issues are far worse than your issues. Today, let's focus on the "Good Times" that are coming, and as long as you hang in there, as long as you continue to believe … you'll be blessed in due season! Okay, I'll leave it alone.

Scripture of the Day:

> And let us not grow weary while doing good, for in due season we shall reap if we do not lose heart.
>
> Galatians 6:9 (NKJV)

The harvest is right there! This is not the time to give up. You may not have seen the harvest up to this point and you may not have gotten that job, yet! You may not have received that lawsuit, yet! You may not have come out of that financial bondage, yet! You may feel as if God has not heard your prayers, but I heard Him say to me through a friend of mine who lives in Boston that "Good Times" are coming! There are better things ahead. Somebody say, "Better things are coming for me!" Okay, I feel a preach coming on. In due season. God is saying that this is the season for you, but you can't lose heart. You're facing your last test, and when you get through this, God is going to have an abundance for you! Somebody shout! Somebody praise Him! If you're sitting at your desk at work, then go in the bathroom or go outside for a couple minutes because this word was for you! Hallelujah! *Good Times*!

"UNSPEAKABLE JOY!"

Somebody needs to get happy this morning! Watch this. In spite of what's going on in your life, you need to get happy because you are about to enter into the joy of the LORD! What's the joy of the LORD? You experience the joy of the LORD when you're able to pay your bills, even if it's not on time. You experience the joy of the LORD when you're able to get out of bed on your own, even when your body aches. You experience the joy of the LORD when you're able to make it, even though you are a single parent. You experience the joy of the LORD when all hell has broken loose in your life and people are laughing at you and gossiping about you, but you keep going to church. You experience the joy of the LORD when you're in your business and the money isn't adding up right and you want to give up and go and work for someone else, but something on the inside makes you keep going back. God spoke to me very early this morning and He said to tell the people that weeping may endure for a night, but here comes joy! And because you have been faithful, He told me to share this with you … read below and then shout! Hallelujah! Sorry, I couldn't wait to read below. I had to shout now because I know He is speaking into my situation as well as yours!

Scripture of the Day:

> His LORD said to him, 'Well done, good and faithful servant; you have been faithful over a few things, I will make you ruler over many things. Enter into the joy of your LORD.'
>
> Matthew 25:23 (NKJV)

Just when you thought the work you were doing for the LORD was going unnoticed, God is saying now is the time to enlarge your territory. You were faithful working in that ministry that seemed like it wasn't going to grow, but now I'm going to enlarge it! You were faithful working at that law firm when the money and the clients weren't coming as fast as you wanted, but God is saying now is the season that you will need an assistant because of all the clients that are coming. You have been faithful over a few things, and now God spoke to me and told me to let you know that you're about to enter into the joy of the LORD! And where the spirit of the LORD is there is liberty! Debt has to let go! Depression has to let go! Poverty has to let go! Somebody needs to shout, "That's for me!" Is there anybody who needs a miracle this morning? And if you do, just say, "I need a miracle!" Now praise Him like it has already taken place. I feel a shift in the Spirit.

THOUGHT OF THE DAY
"IT'S EITHER THIS OR THAT. IT'S UP TO YOU!"

Today, I just wanted to tell you that I know it's hard. I know it's difficult. Life has dealt you some circumstances and situations that make you ask the question, "why me?" But I want to tell you that the choice is yours as to which way you will go. God can only show you the way. You have to choose the way. You can only blame yourself if you fail. We can't blame our neighbors, we can't blame our jobs, we can't blame the church, we can't blame the Pastor, we can't even blame the haters because God has given us the instructions on how to get to glory. Since we have the instructions, we become liable for getting there. When you buy a new bicycle, it usually comes in a box with various pieces and instructions. In order to put the bike together, you not only need the instructions, but you need the correct tools! You see, God has given you the right instructions and now you need to bring the right praise! You need to bring the right attitude! You need to worship Him in spirit and in truth. It is up to you. Start your praise this morning to let God know that you have chosen the correct way! Praise Him!

Scripture of the Day:

> If they obey and serve Him, They shall spend their days in prosperity, And their years in pleasures. But if they do not obey, They shall perish by the sword, And they shall die without knowledge.
>
> Job 36:11–12 (NKJV)

If you want to spend your days in peace, if you want to spend your days with joy, if you want to be prosperous in these last days, then you need to obey Him! If you do not obey Him, then you will suffer the rest of your days. God does not want this to happen to you. He does not want you to suffer and die without knowledge. This is why He has given us the instructions. You must decide which way you want to go. You have to obey the LORD and trust in the LORD. He is with you every step of the way. God is with you in every situation you deal with. Psalms says He is a very present help in time of trouble. Listen. He's in your troubles before you get in them! You need to start praising right now before anything happens. Praise Him today… Praise Him today and let God know that He's worthy to be praised! Lift your hands in the sanctuary—and that can be wherever you are because we can praise the LORD anywhere. Don't be ashamed. Praise Him!

"IT'S YOURS IF YOU WANT IT!"

Let's rejoice because this is the day the LORD has made for us. There is no need to complain because you're at work. Listen. There are some people who would love to switch places with you. They would love to take on your issues while you take on their issues, so just give the LORD praise right now and for the fact that you have life today! I will be very brief today. God put this on my heart last week. Are you ready? There are two things you need to do today. First, you need to pray because the Bible says to pray without ceasing. We must always be praying. Second, while you are praying, you need to have praise. Why? Prayer is communication with God. You are actually telling Him what you need. Praise says to God that what you have just prayed for is already done! Somebody missed that! Pray and then praise God!

Scripture of the Day:

> Therefore, I say to you, whatever things you ask when you pray, believe that you receive them, and you will have them.
>
> Mark 11:24 (NKJV)

Read that again, please! Christ is speaking in this scripture. Whatever you ask for when you pray, already believe you have received it and you will have it! I'm going to end right here. Pray and then praise!

THOUGHT OF THE DAY
"YOU'RE IN LABOR!"

This is not the season to give up! That has been in my heart all week. I'm praying someone will catch this. This is not the time to throw in the towel. All odds are against you, but God is saying now is the appointed time for your breakthrough. All hell has broken loose in your life, but God is saying now is the time for the appointed breakthrough. You're about to go into labor. Turn to your neighbor and say, "I think my water just broke!" In a pregnancy, when the water breaks it means it's time to give birth to your miracle. In the spiritual realm, the water symbolizes praise and when your praise breaks loose that means it's time for God to birth the miracle inside you. Can I get a witness? In labor, you'll experience pain. The discomfort will make you uneasy. The pain will be unbearable, but you have to go through it to give birth. God is saying, "Don't abort your blessing!" You've come to far now to give up. You've gone through too much hell to give in now. Get what belongs to you. Birth your blessing! This is the season to reap if you do not faint. Somebody needs to give God crazy praise because you're about to give birth to a crazy blessing!

Scripture of the Day:

> And let us not grow weary while doing good, for in due season we shall reap if we do not lose heart.
>
> Galatians 6:9 (NKJV)

You didn't receive it last year because it wasn't the season; you didn't receive it last month because it wasn't the season, but God is saying now is the time! If you had tried to give birth to it back then it would have been a premature blessing. In other words, it wouldn't have been fully developed. It took some time to be developed, and through that time God sustained you. He didn't allow you to go under. He kept you afloat until now! (I'm about to shout!) When a woman is overdue in her pregnancy, the doctor usually performs a C-section, which means they go in and take the baby out. God is about to perform a spiritual C-section on you; the blessing is overdue, the miracle is overdue, your season is overdue, so God is going to go in and take the blessing out of you! His promises are coming to pass and no weapon formed against you shall be able to prosper. Somebody better come and stop me! Get ready! Get ready! The season is now and God is about to bless you with something that eyes have not seen and ears have not heard. You're going to be the first with whatever God blesses you with. I have to leave this alone or I'll start preaching! Somebody just shout, "I'm in labor!"

THOUGHT OF THE DAY
"PETTY THINGS!"

Today is a little different. There is no Scripture reference today. However, that doesn't mean that this word is not from the LORD. God showed me something last night to share with you today. Here we go. Right now, many of you are at the point of your breakthrough. You are that close to your miracle. You are on the very edge of stepping into your season. Guess what's holding you back? Okay, guess again. Petty things! Here's what I mean. You don't talk with your closest friend any longer because someone else started a rumor, gossip, or lies and that split you two apart. Your boss or coworker got on your nerves, so now you act differently towards them. You walk into work and speak to everyone except them. Maybe your spouse said something and you're waiting for them to apologize, but they are probably waiting on you to say something. Petty things! Let me ask you this question. What if you refused to speak to someone and, God forbid, something happens to them? How would you feel? How would you feel knowing that the last thing that occurred between you and the other person was something petty! You would have to live the rest of your life knowing that you wanted to apologize, but you couldn't because the person is gone!

Thought of a Lifetime:

"Do not allow the enemy make you go to sleep without asking for forgiveness from both the LORD and people!"

Petty things! Don't allow things that are truly petty to hinder you from your breakthrough. God told me to let someone know that you're that close to your miracle but because of petty things, you're slowing down the process. I don't know about you, but I don't want to miss out on what God has for me, especially because of someone else. Let's drop the pride and get what God has for us! Pray for me and I'll pray for you!

THOUGHT OF THE DAY
"LOOK FOR THE CHAOS!"

Today I want you to focus on the chaos! Hold on before you hit delete. Here's what God shared with me today. God told me to let you know that He has plans for your life. He desires to bless you and to make you prosperous and debt free. He wants to deliver you from that situation and remove the curse that has been placed on your life. He wants to restore the years that you have lost and what the enemy has taken from you, but every time God gets ready to move, you miss the mark because of the people you are dealing with, the company you keep, and your circle of so-called friends. And let me share this: all of the people around you aren't praying for your good. Some are there just to make sure you don't get that new house. They are there just to make sure you don't get married. They want you to be just as miserable as them. You know the saying, "Misery loves company." Have you noticed that people who are miserable can't be alone? The reason is they want others

to get caught up in their mess. Today, look for the chaos
and when you find it, run!

Scripture of the Day:

> For where envy and self-seeking exist, confusion
> and every evil thing are there.
>
> James 3:16 (NKJV)

Somebody read that again so it gets in your spirit! There
are people around you that literally pray that you don't get
to preach at the Sunday service. They pray that you don't
get that promotion. They pray God uses them and not you.
This is called envy, and when folk get envious of you, they
will do anything to try and stop the move of God in your
life, but God has given us a sign to look for. We serve a God
of order, and if you see a bunch of confusion and mess, it's
not of God! If this is taking place, then check the people
around you and do a spiritual ultrasound to see what's on
the inside. If there's jealousy, envy, and strife, then remove
yourself because you better believe every evil thing is in their
presence. Check for the chaos and if you sense it, then make
a power move because God said to let you know that the
chaos is the very thing that's holding you back from your
breakthrough! So move, get out the way!

THOUGHT OF THE DAY
"THE RETURN OF THE HATER!"

Give God a praise before you read this! He woke you up this morning! Today, many of you are at the point of your breakthrough. You are right at the edge and Here's how you can tell. All hell has broken out in your life. You are having money problems like never before. All of a sudden, your health is being attacked. Your children are acting strange. The people in your church are bugging out. It seems like no matter what you do, there is opposition. That is a sign of a breakthrough. However, we look at opposition and get frustrated or distracted, which is its intention, but the devil is a liar! All those who are praying against you, plotting against you, laughing and smiling in your face and at the same time planning a way to take you out; all those who are trying to get close to your spouse, who are going to leaders in the church making false accusations, who are going to lunch with you on your job but are trying to get your position; all these folks who are just plain-ole hating on you … guess what? They are coming back to bless you. They are going to be the ones who get you over that hump of your breakthrough, but you have to pray in the spirit and not allow your flesh to react! We do not wrestle against flesh and blood, but against spiritual wickedness in high places.

Scripture of the Day:

> Also the sons of those who afflicted you Shall come bowing to you, And all those who despised you shall fall prostrate at the soles of your feet; And they shall call you The City of the LORD, Zion of the Holy One of Israel. Whereas you have been forsaken and hated, So that no one went through you, I will make you an eternal excellence, A joy of many generations.
>
> Isaiah 60:14–15 (NKJV)

The Bible says that God will make your enemies your footstool. They will assist you in going higher. They are coming back to a theater near you! The haters are coming back and they will be bowing to you. God is going to make you excellent. He's going to perfect the ministry He gave you, and those who gave up on your ministry will have to see the gratification of it! They walked out on you, but God will put them back in place to see you rising up in Him! The haters are going to fall prostrate at your feet. They are going to be the last piece of the puzzle that you needed to complete your breakthrough. So, there's no need for you to hate on them because they are hating on you, just thank the LORD, pray, and move on. God will deal with them. Remember they really aren't hating on you anyway. Instead, the forces of evil are trying to prevail. Listen. Have you noticed lately that even those who were once for you are now coming against you? That should let you know how close you truly are!